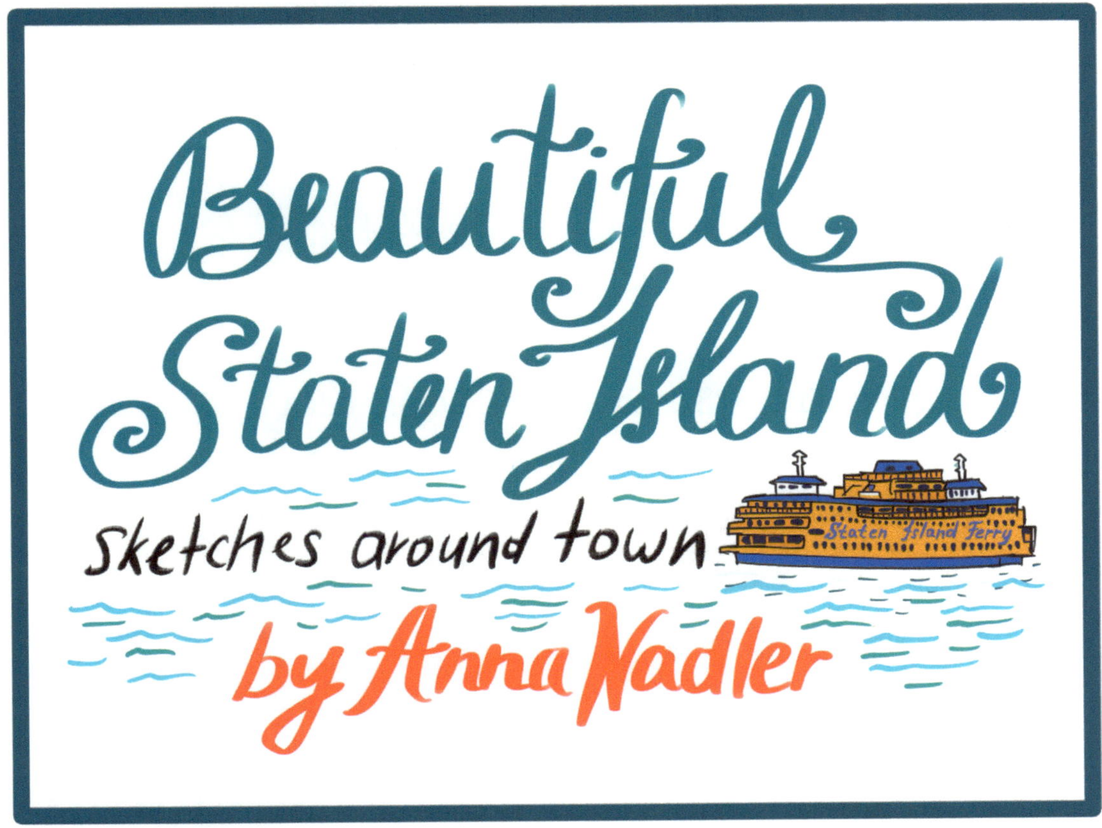

ISBN: 9781958428023

Dedication

For Stevie, who is always there for me.

Acknowledgments

This book and the "Staten Island Coloring Book" were made
possible by a DCA Premier Grant from Staten Island Arts,
with public funding from the New York City Department
of Cultural Affairs.

Description

This is a collection of drawings from my several sketchbooks,
which I wanted to publish and dedicate to the borough I love -
Beautiful Staten Island.

Each sketch in this book was created on location. Location sketches
are designed to capture the immediate feeling of the places. The lines are
spontaneous and quick. Some drawings were done in color, some in
black and white. Materials used were pens, markers, watercolors
graphite, and color pencils.

Thank you for getting this book, I hope you enjoy it!

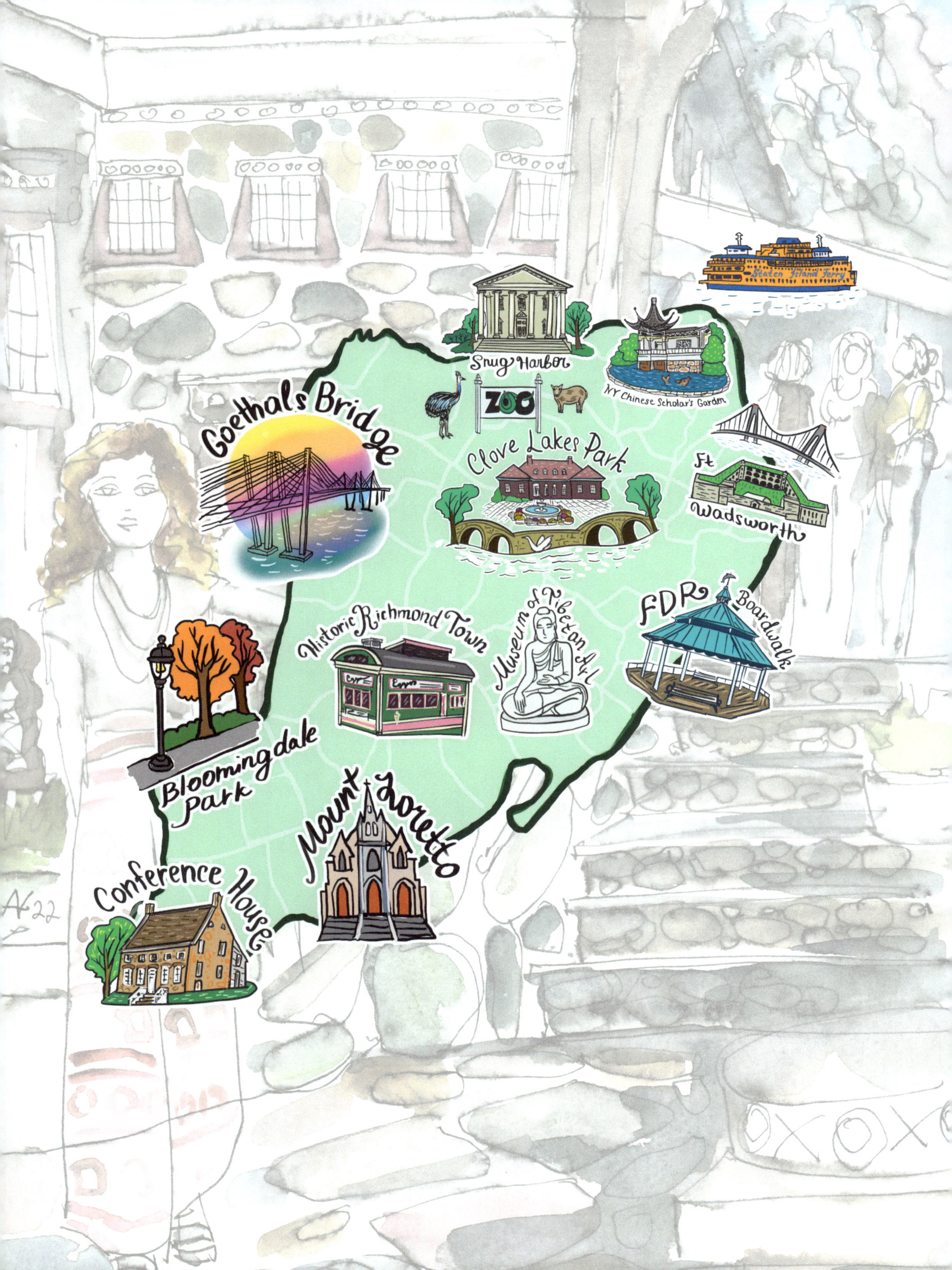

Staten Island Ferry
Snug Harbor
ZOO
NY Chinese Scholar's Garden
Goethals Bridge
Clove Lakes Park
Ft Wadsworth
Historic Richmond Town
Museum of Tibetan Art
FDR Boardwalk
Bloomingdale Park
Mount Loretto
Conference House
A22

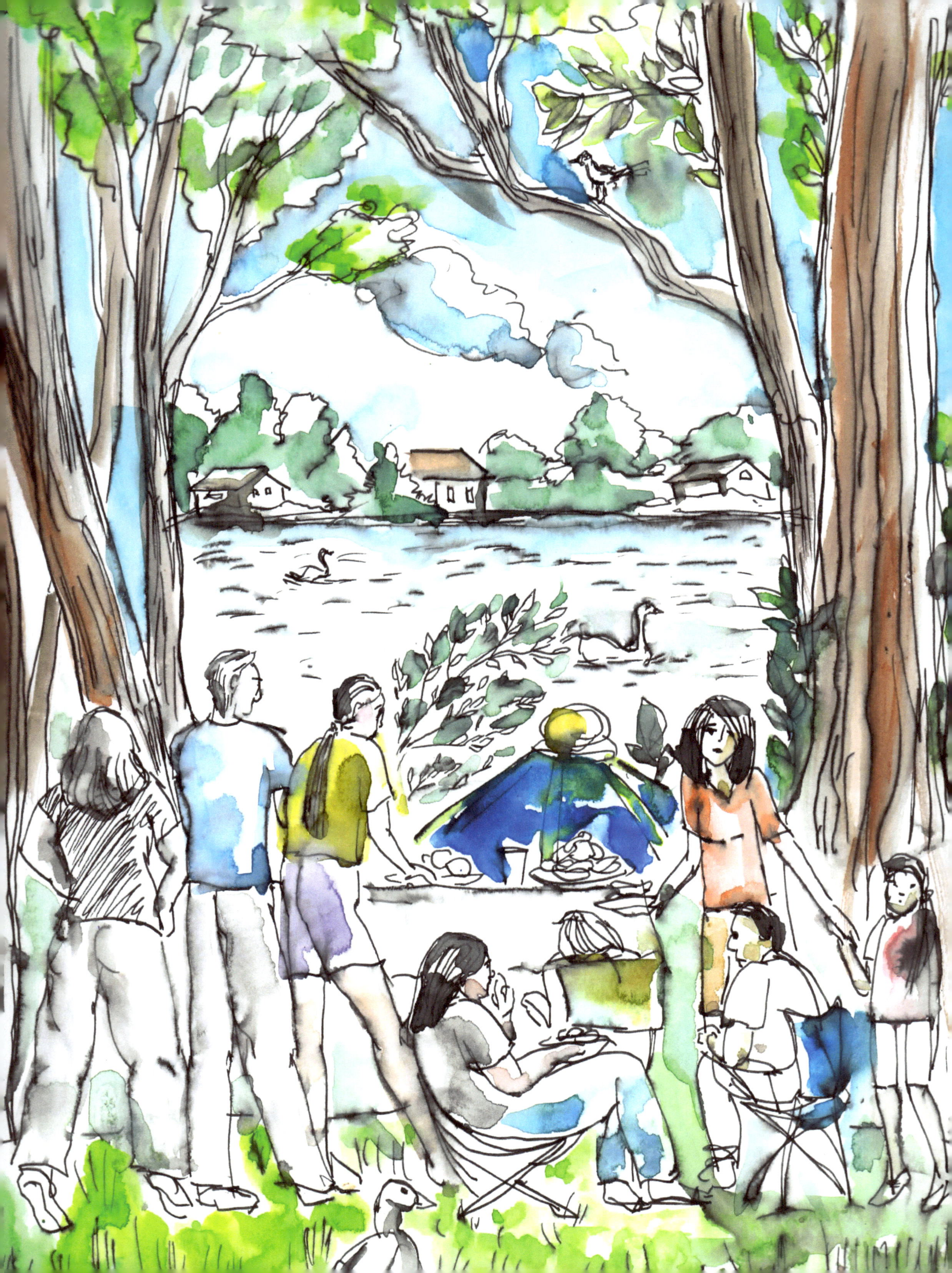

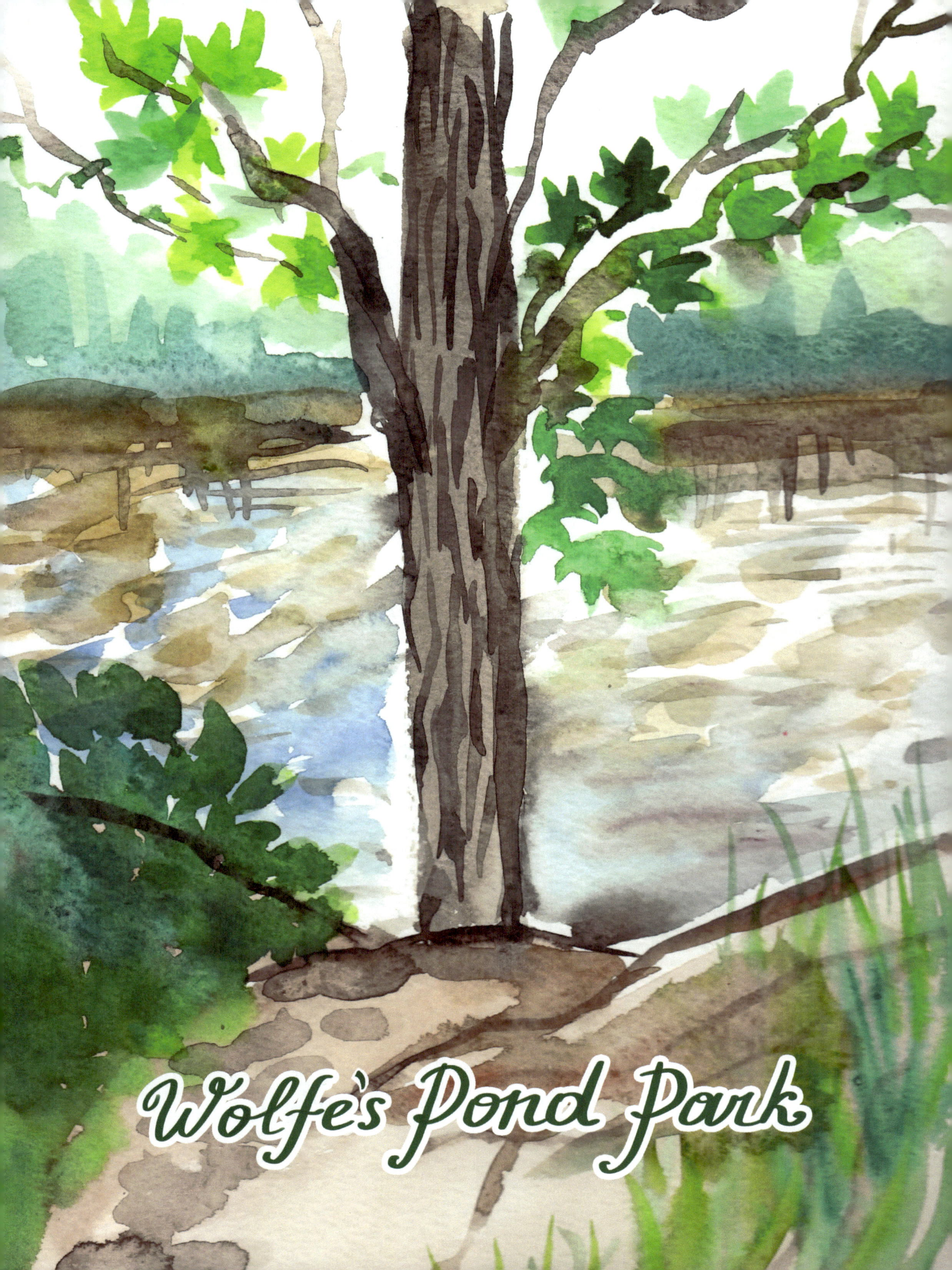
Wolfe's Pond Park

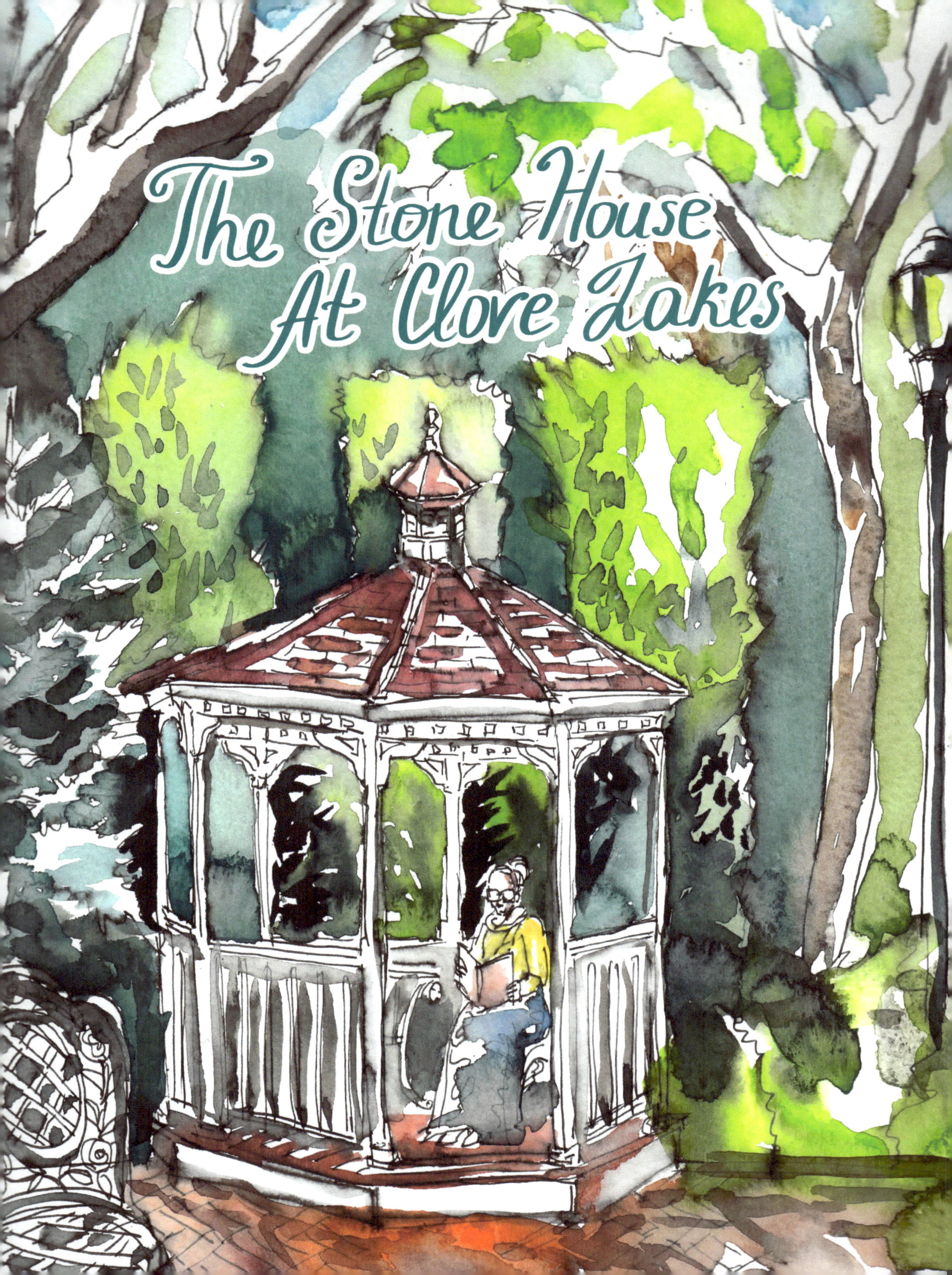

The Stone House
At Clove Lakes

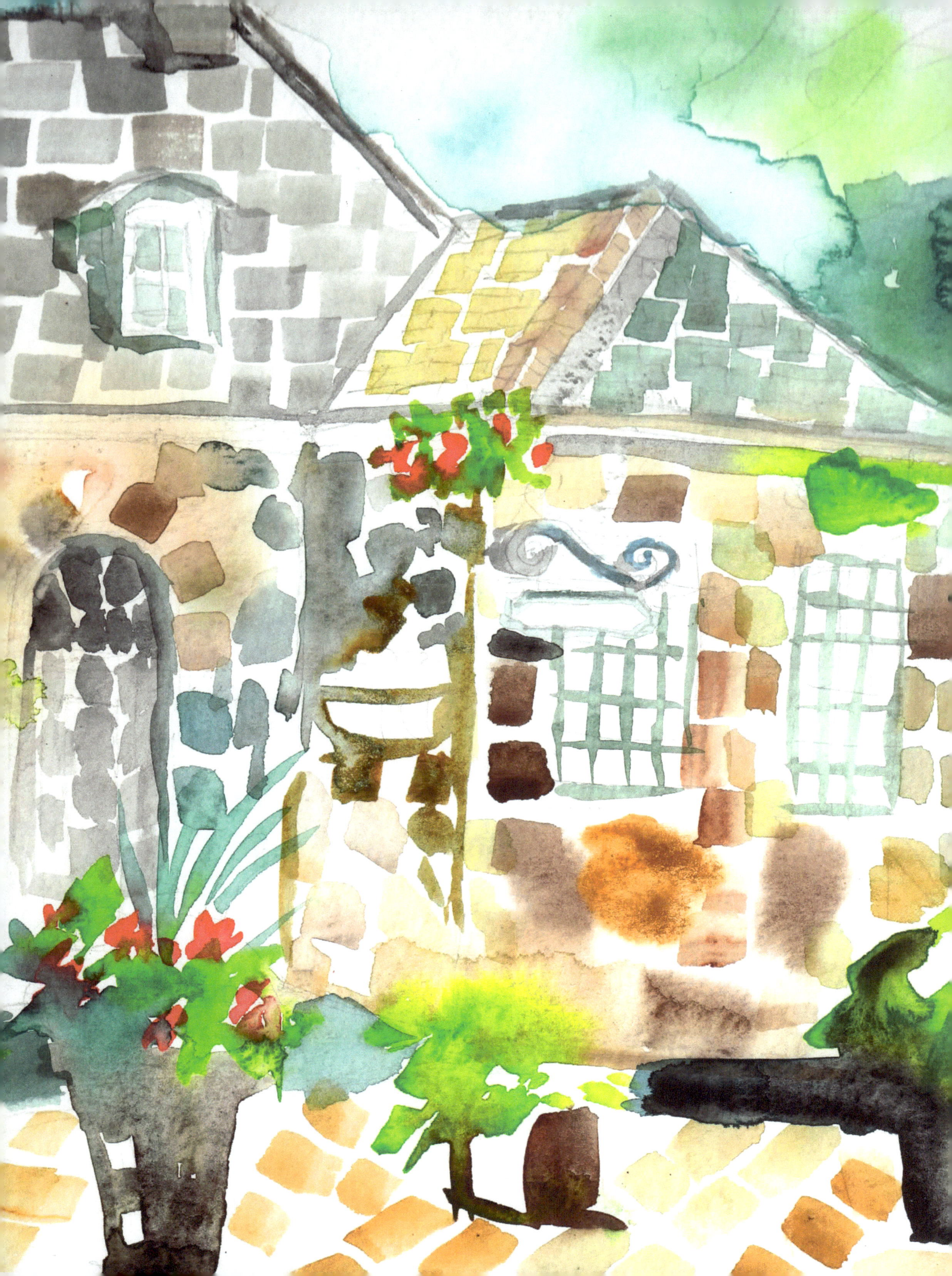

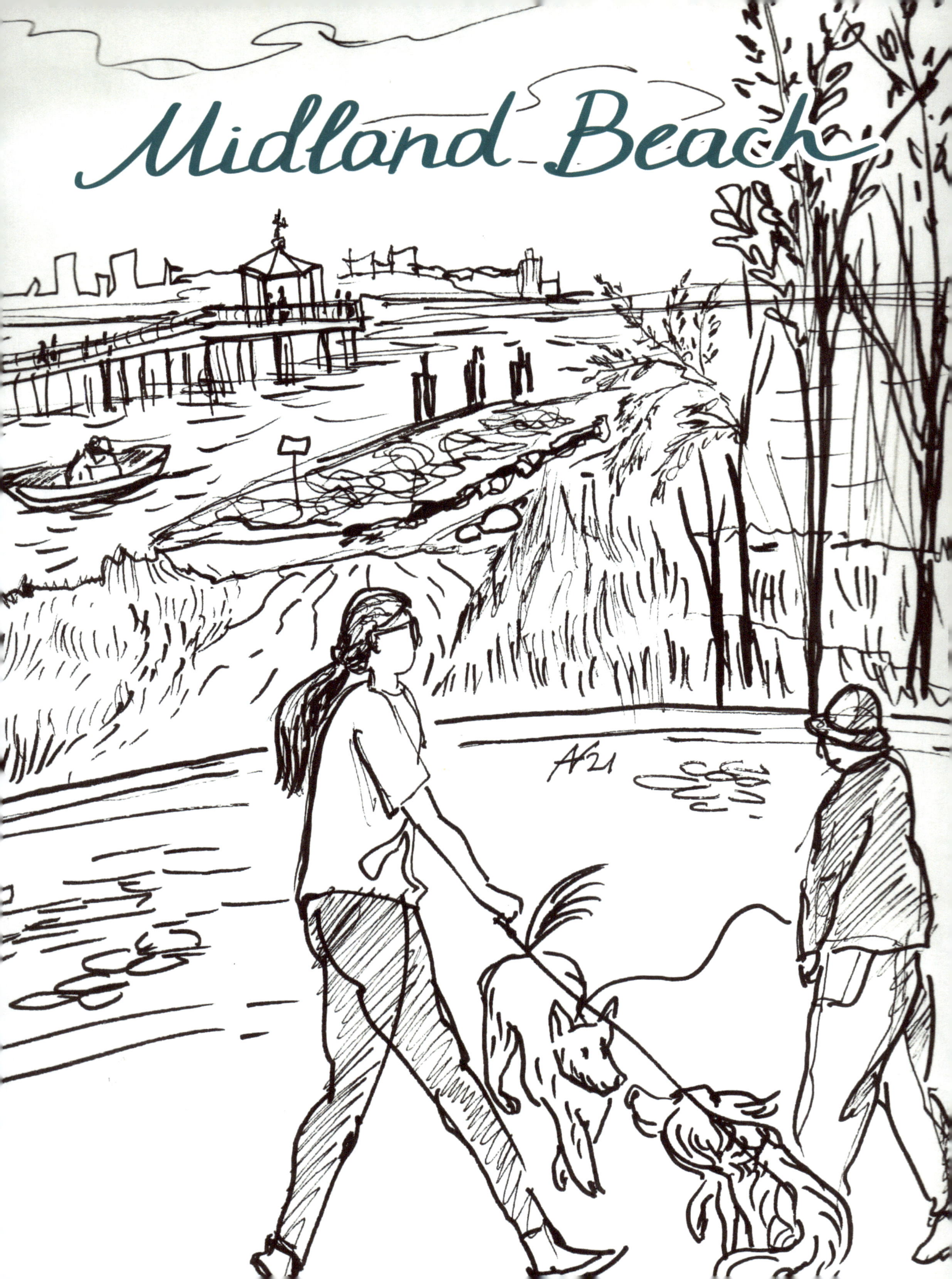

Midland Beach

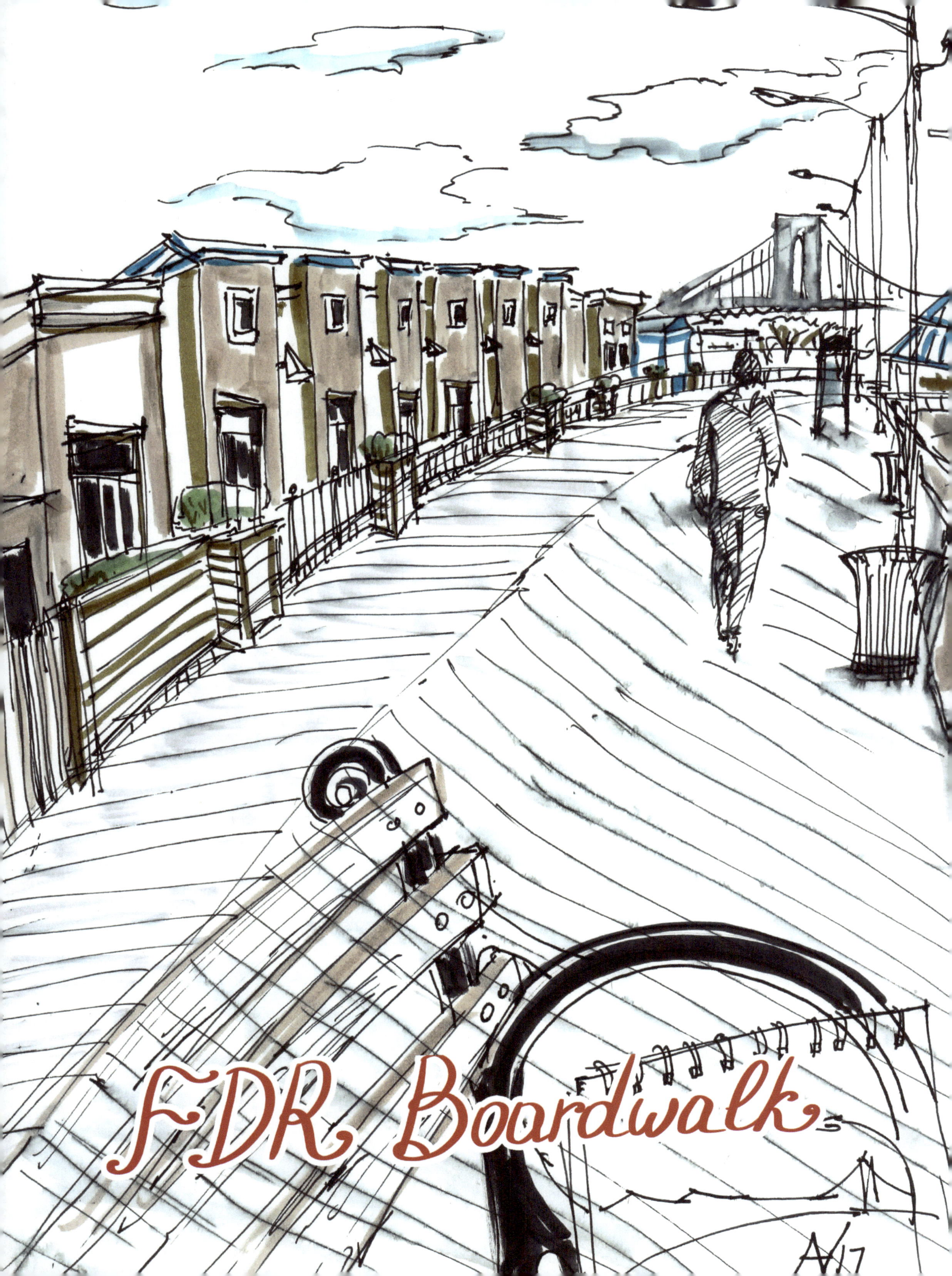

FDR Boardwalk
A/17

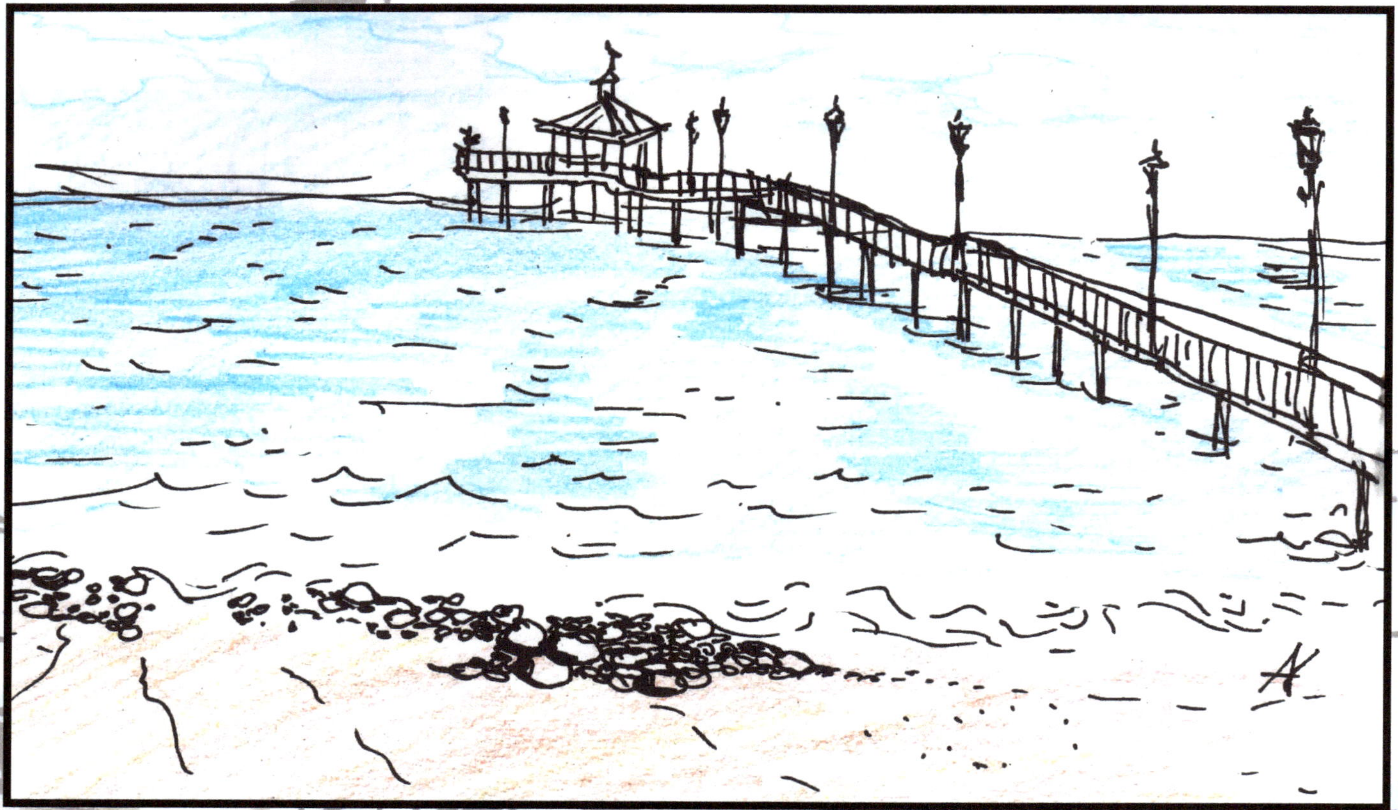

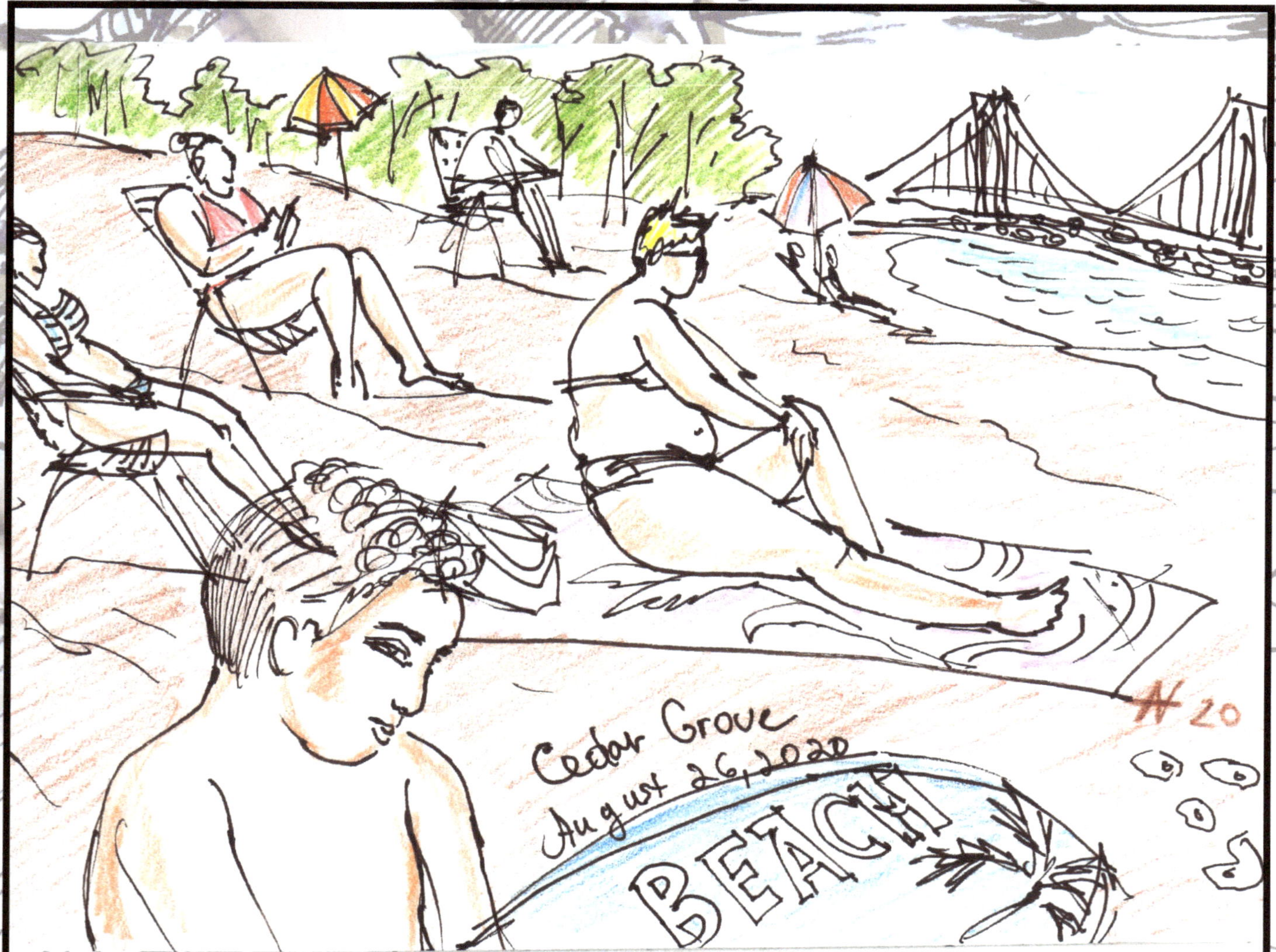

Cedar Grove
August 26, 2020
BEACH

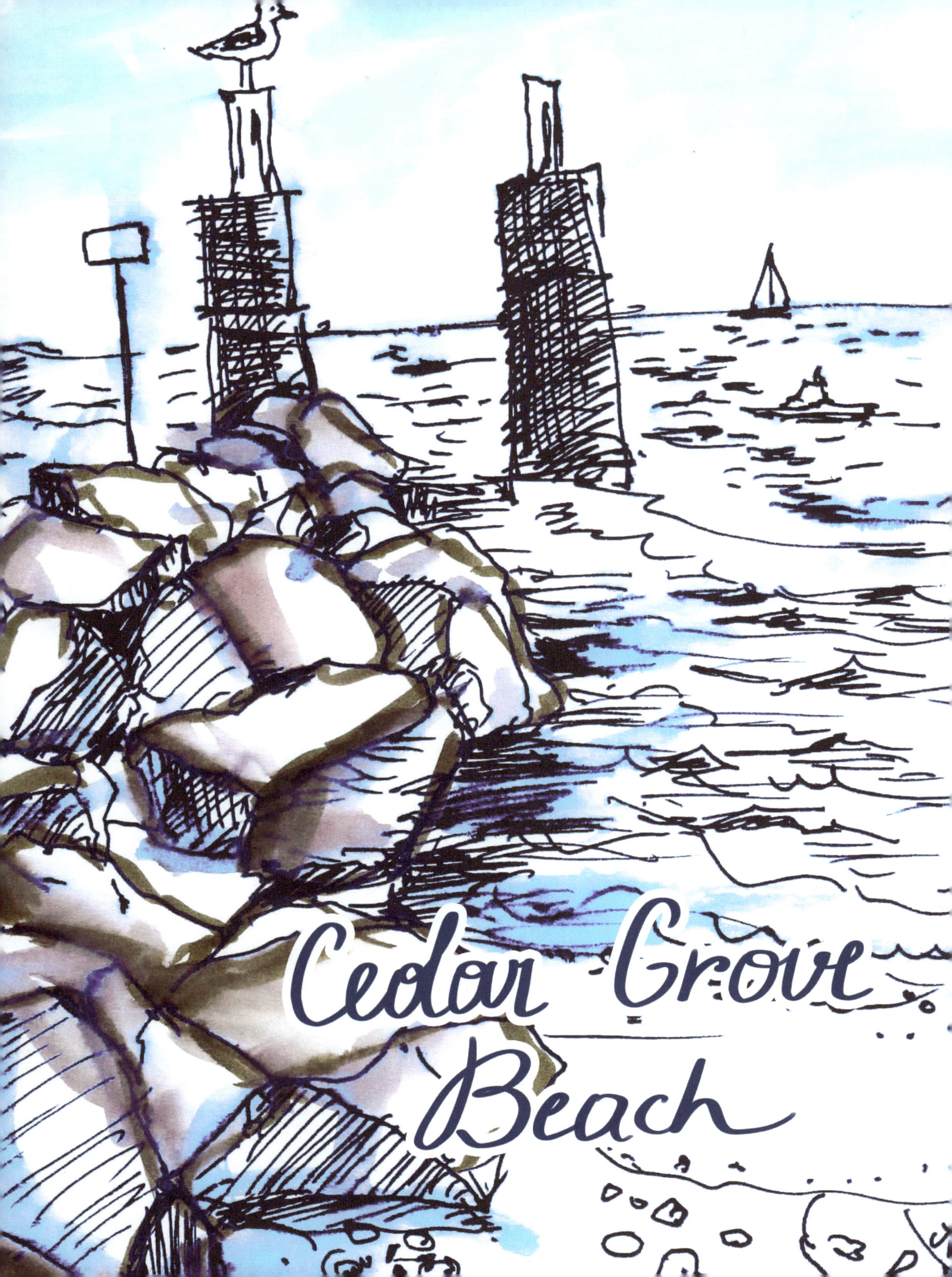
Cedar Grove
Beach

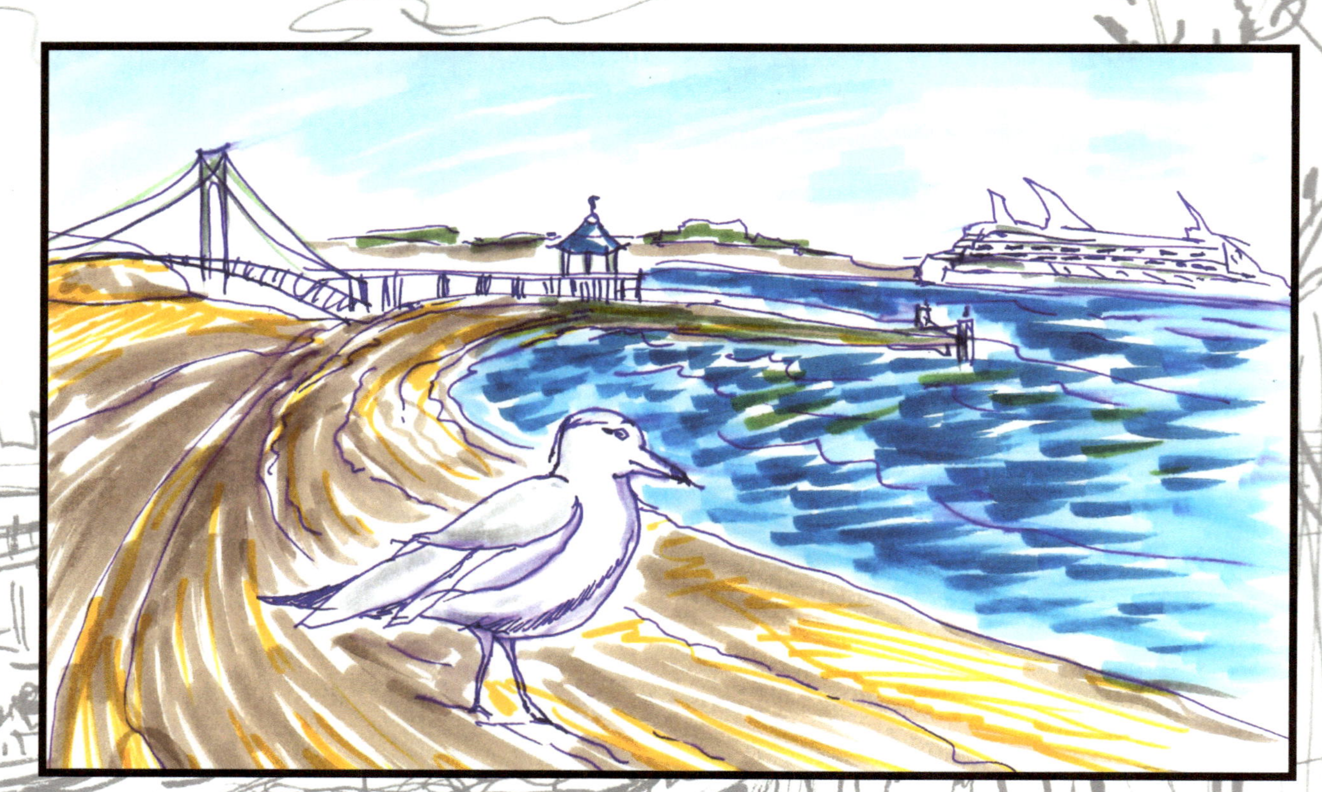

Turtle Fountain

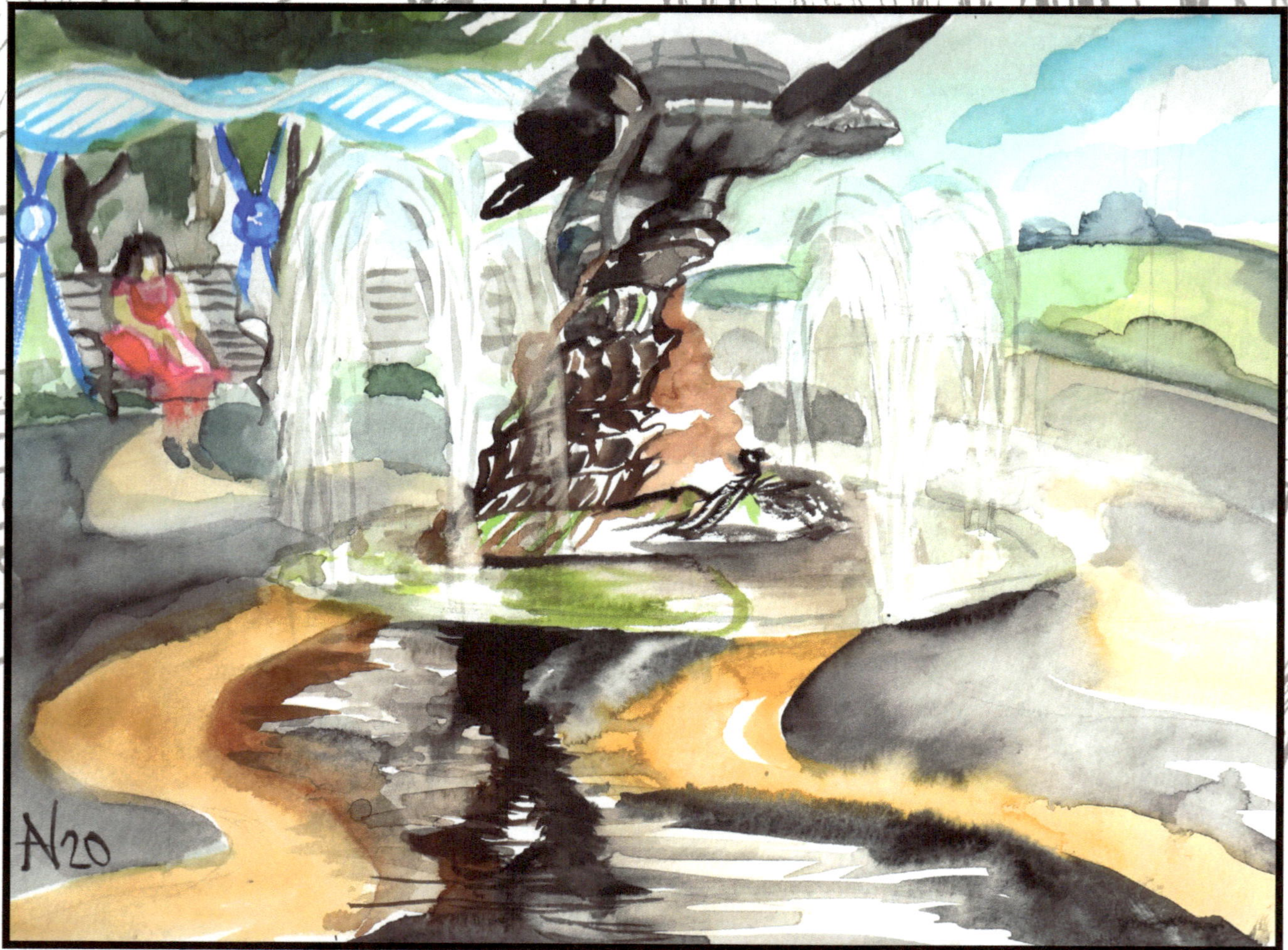

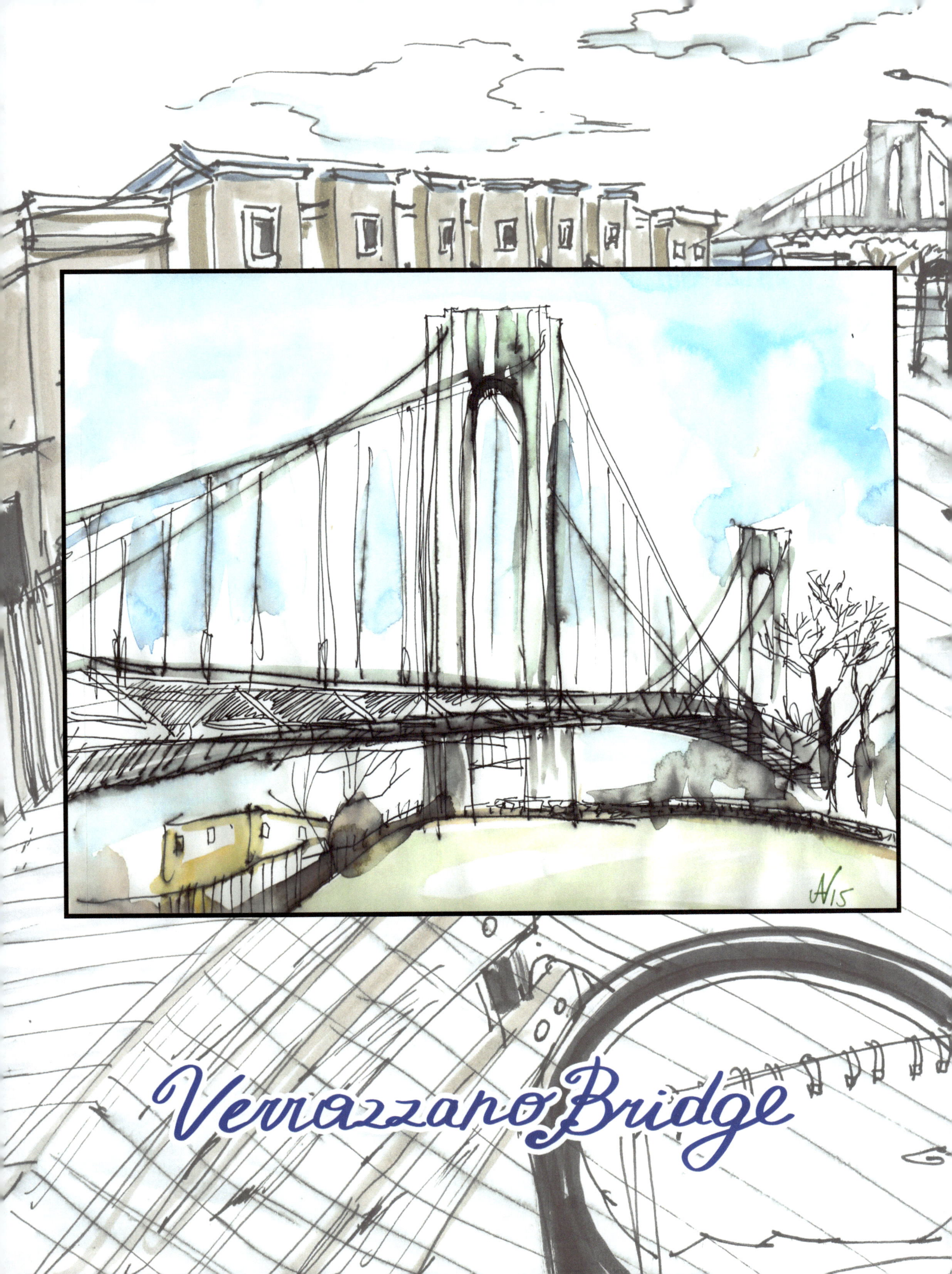

Verrazzano Bridge

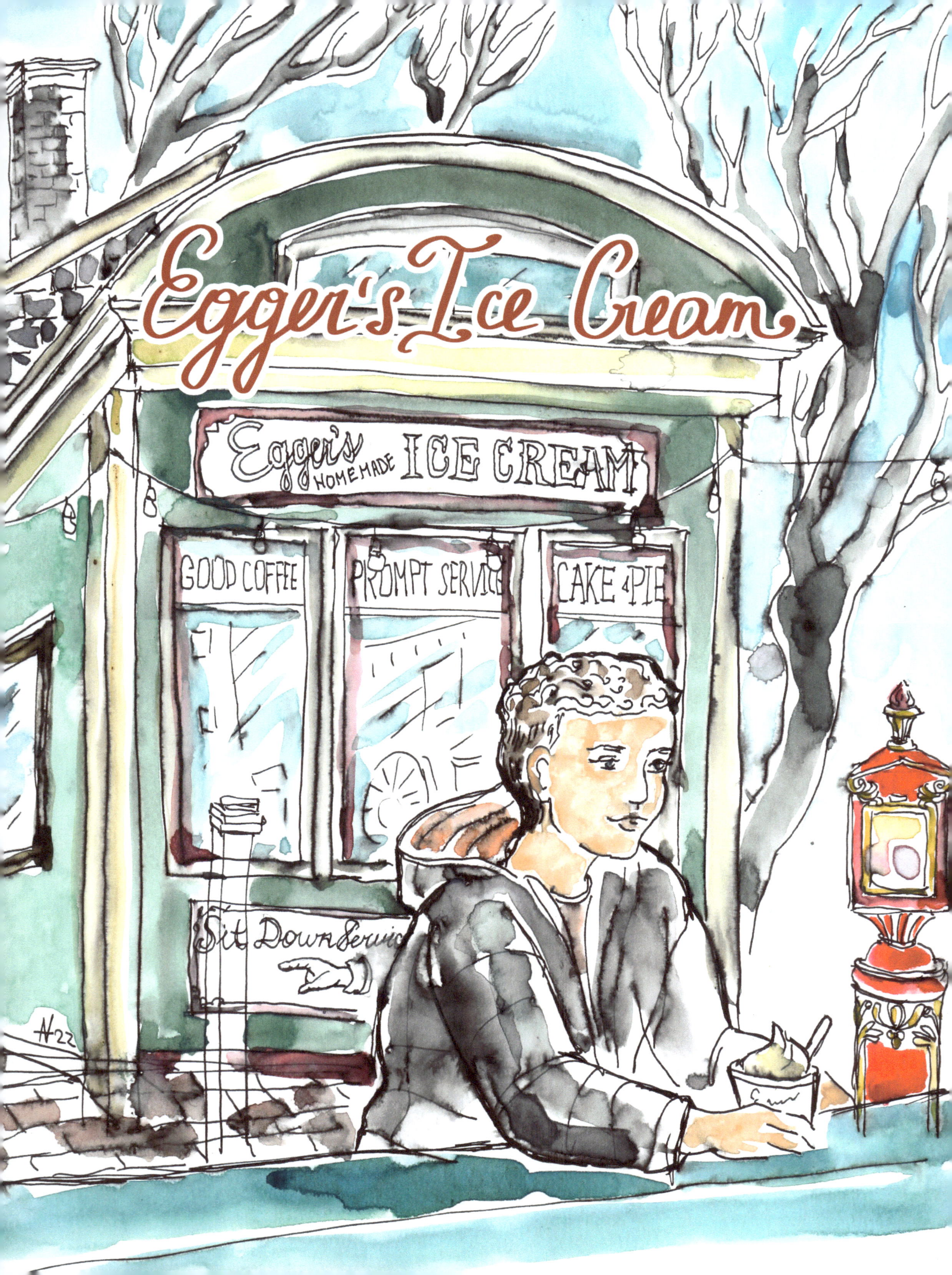

Egger's Ice Cream
Egger's HOMEMADE ICE CREAM
GOOD COFFEE
PROMPT SERVICE
CAKE & PIE
Sit Down Service

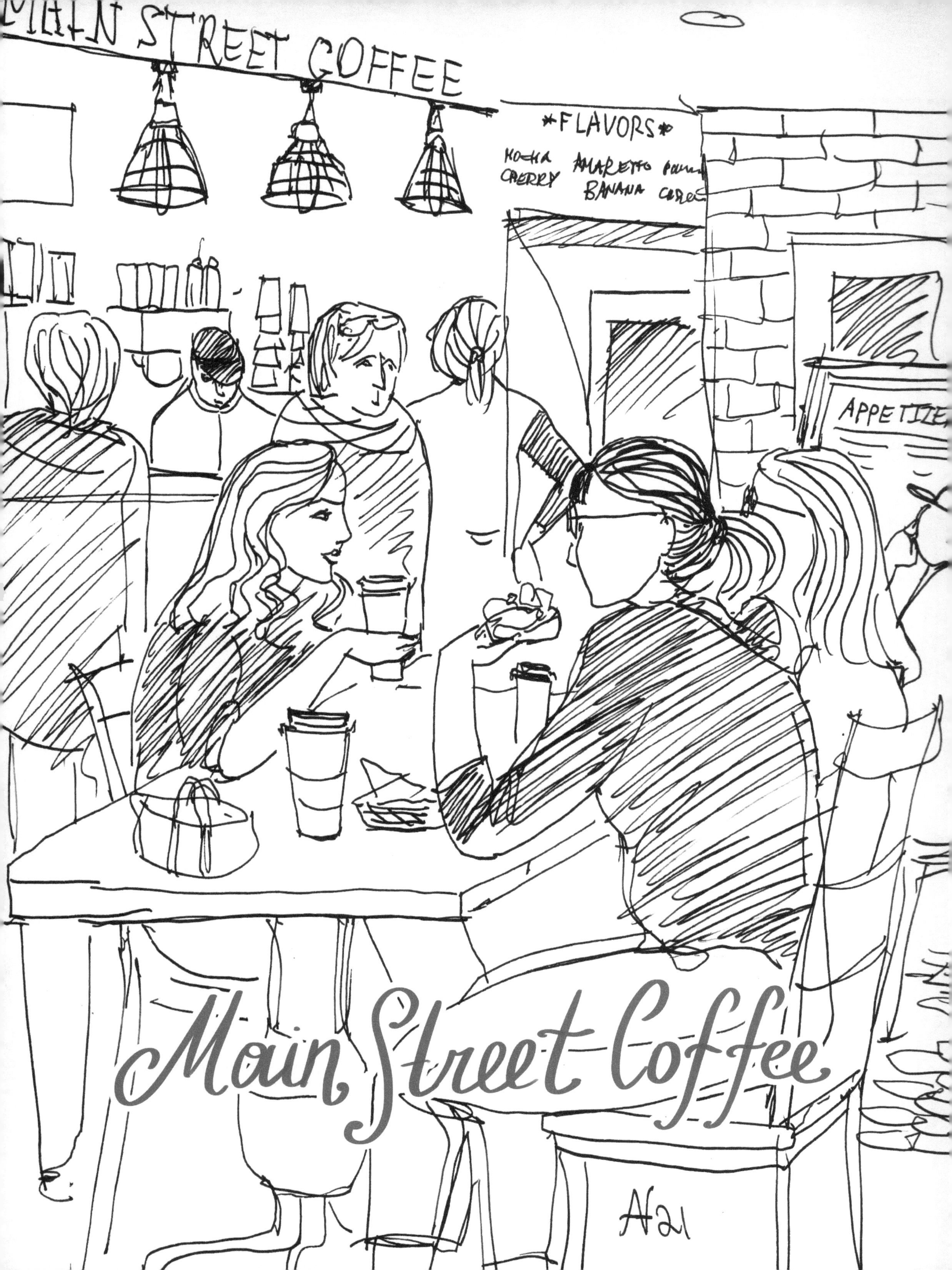

MAIN STREET COFFEE
FLAVORS
MOCHA
CHERRY   AMARETTO
BANANA
APPETIZE
Main Street Coffee
A 21

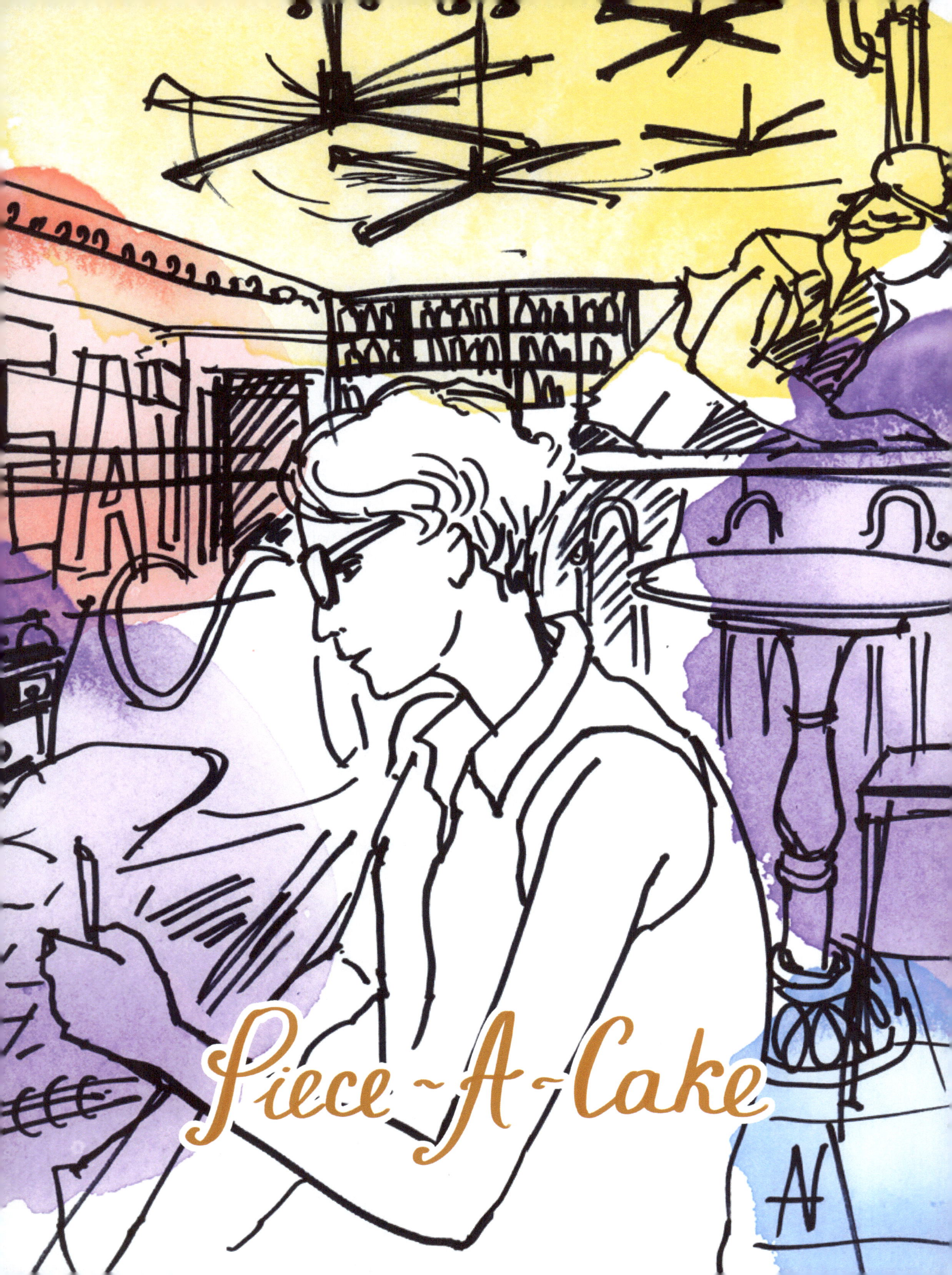

Piece-A-Cake

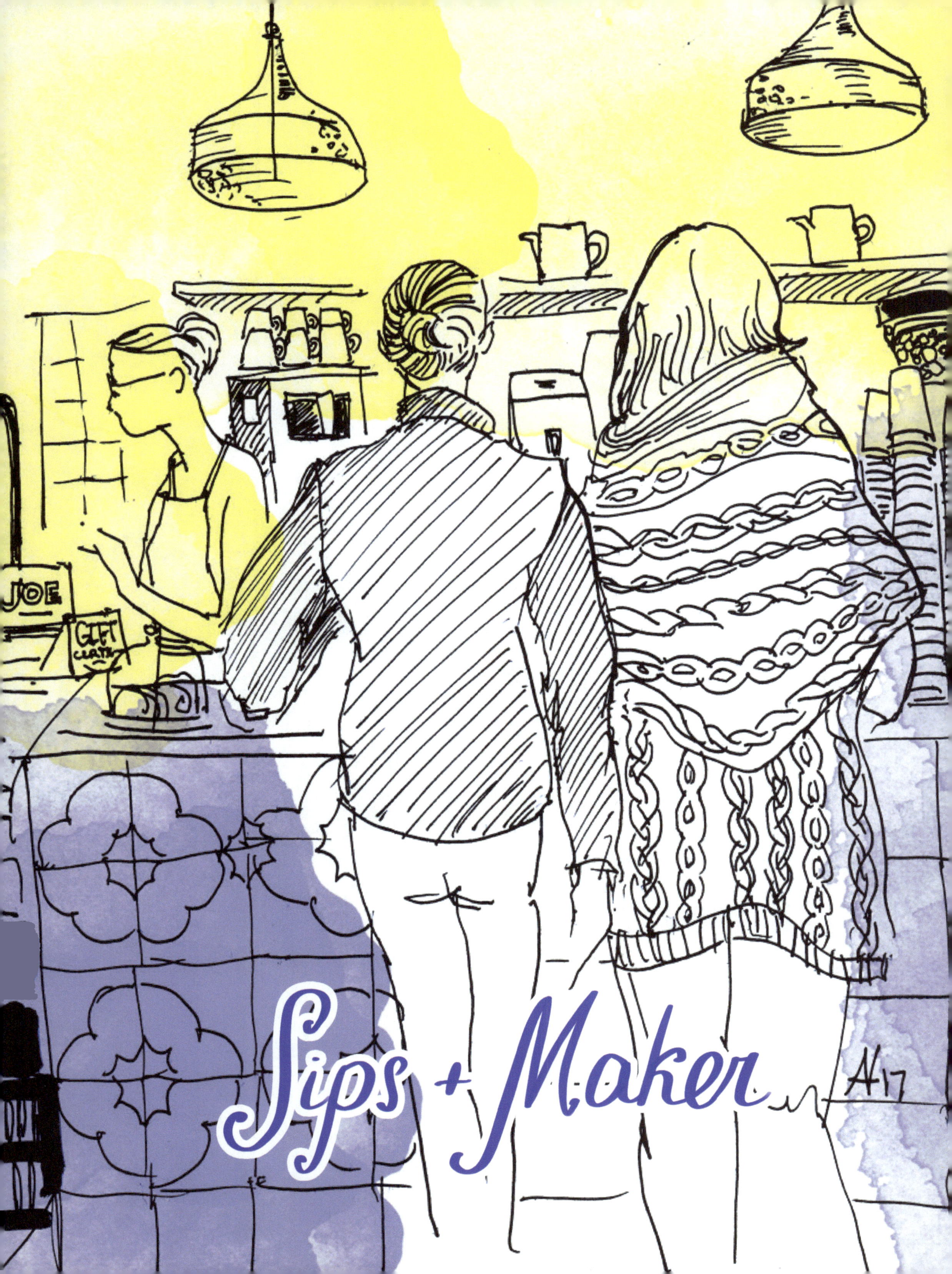

JOE
GIFT CARDS
Sips + Maker
A17

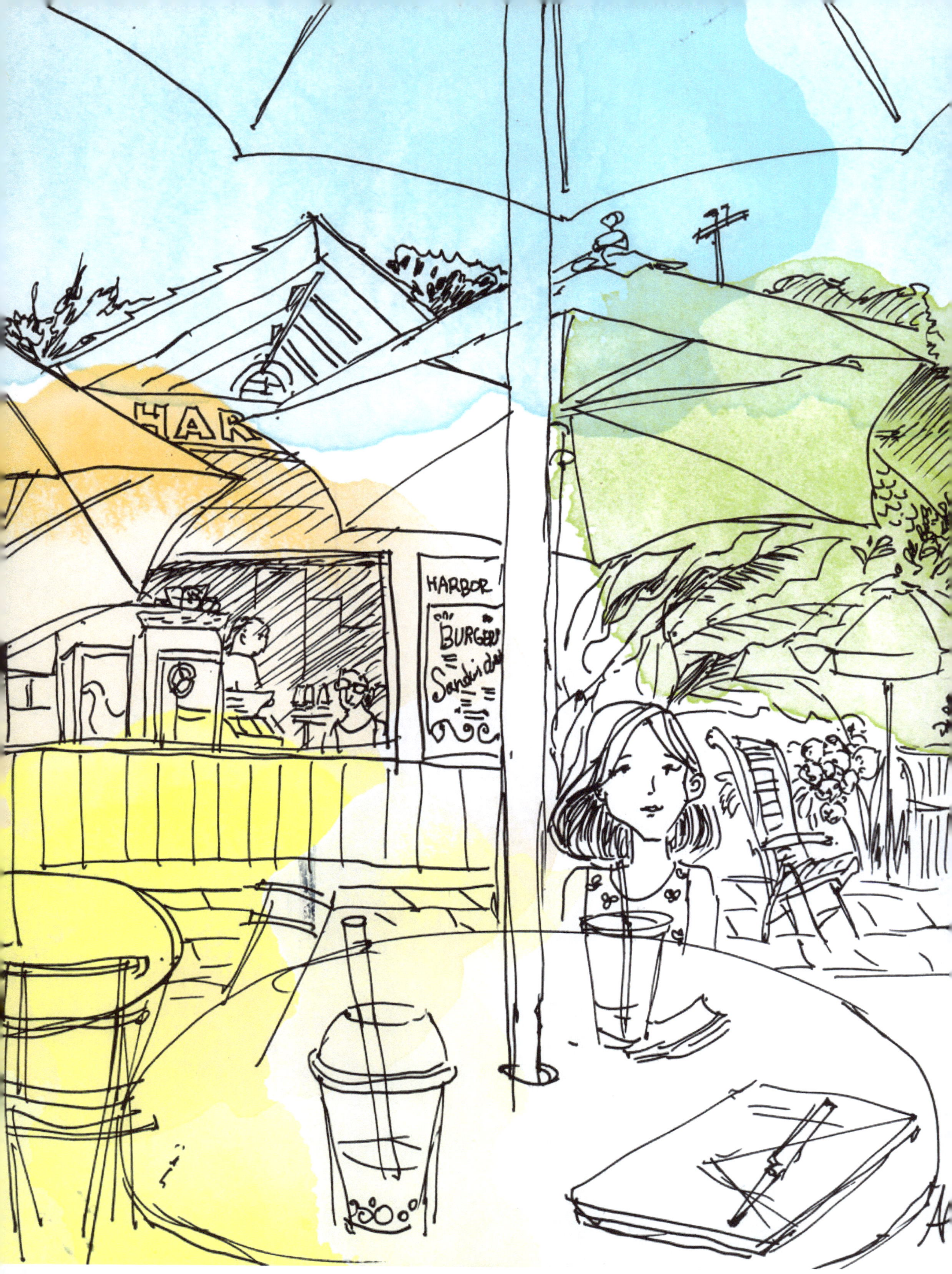
HAR
HARBOR
BURGERS
Sandwiches

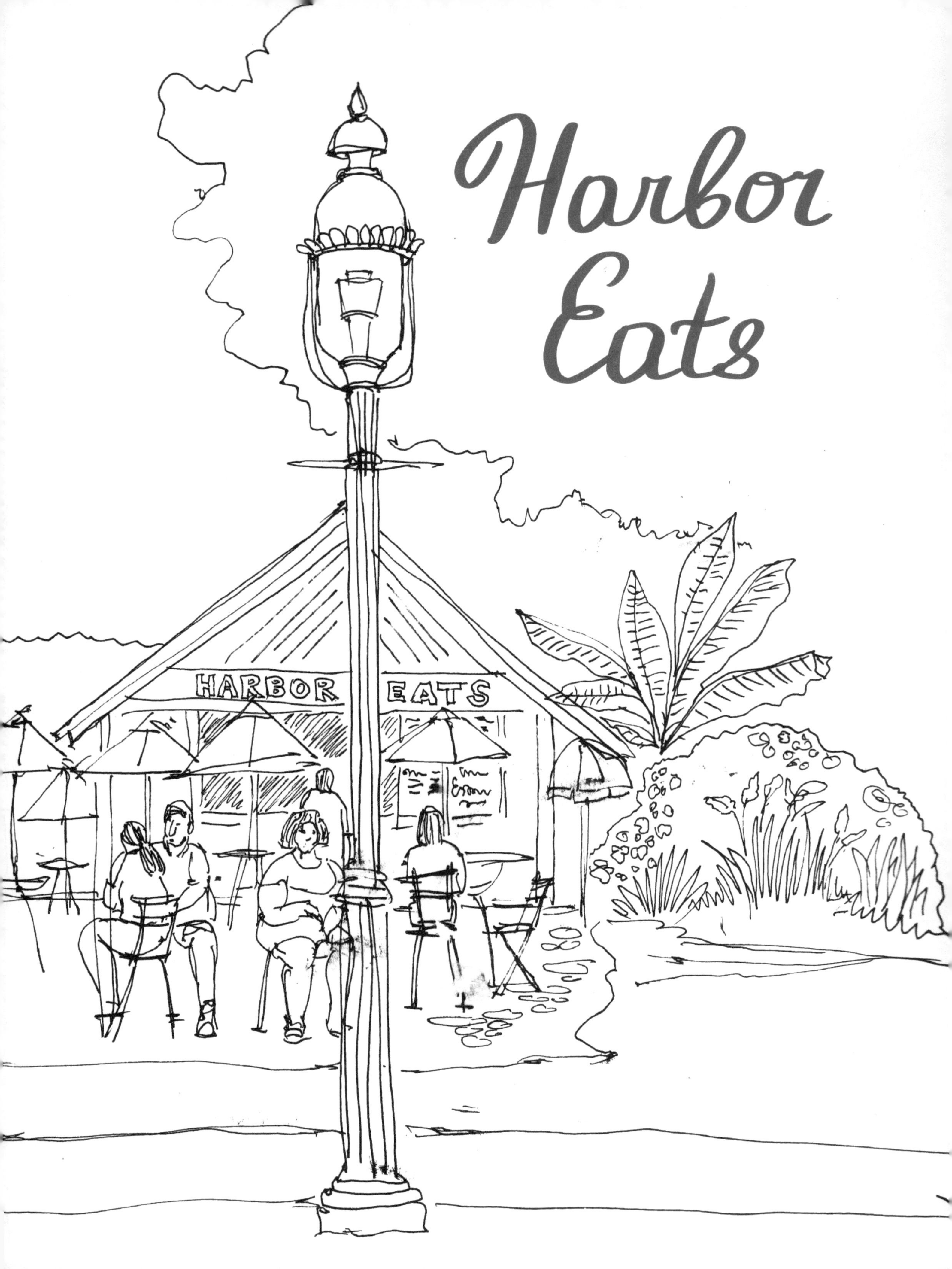

Harbor
Eats
HARBOR EATS

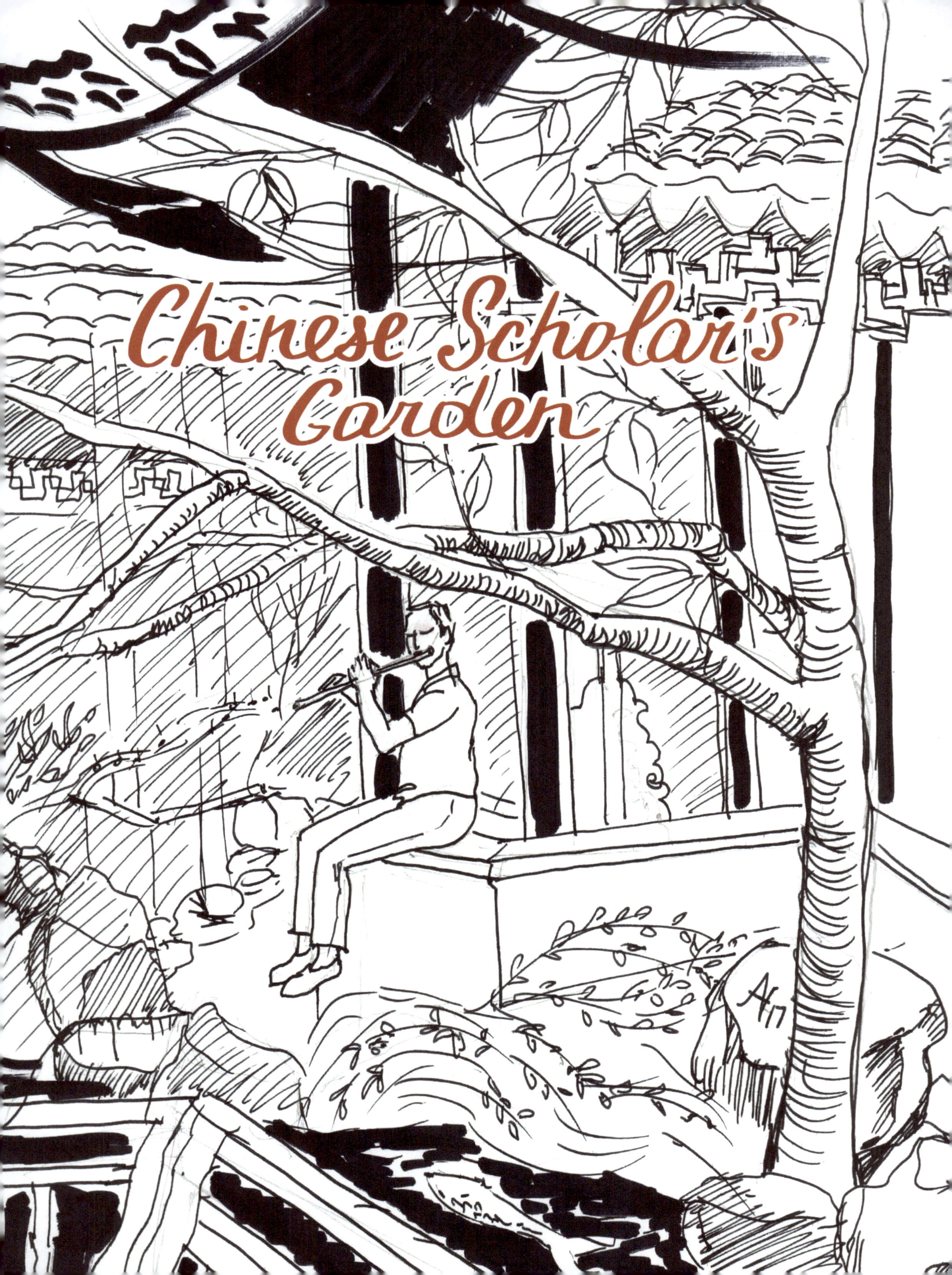

Chinese Scholar's Garden

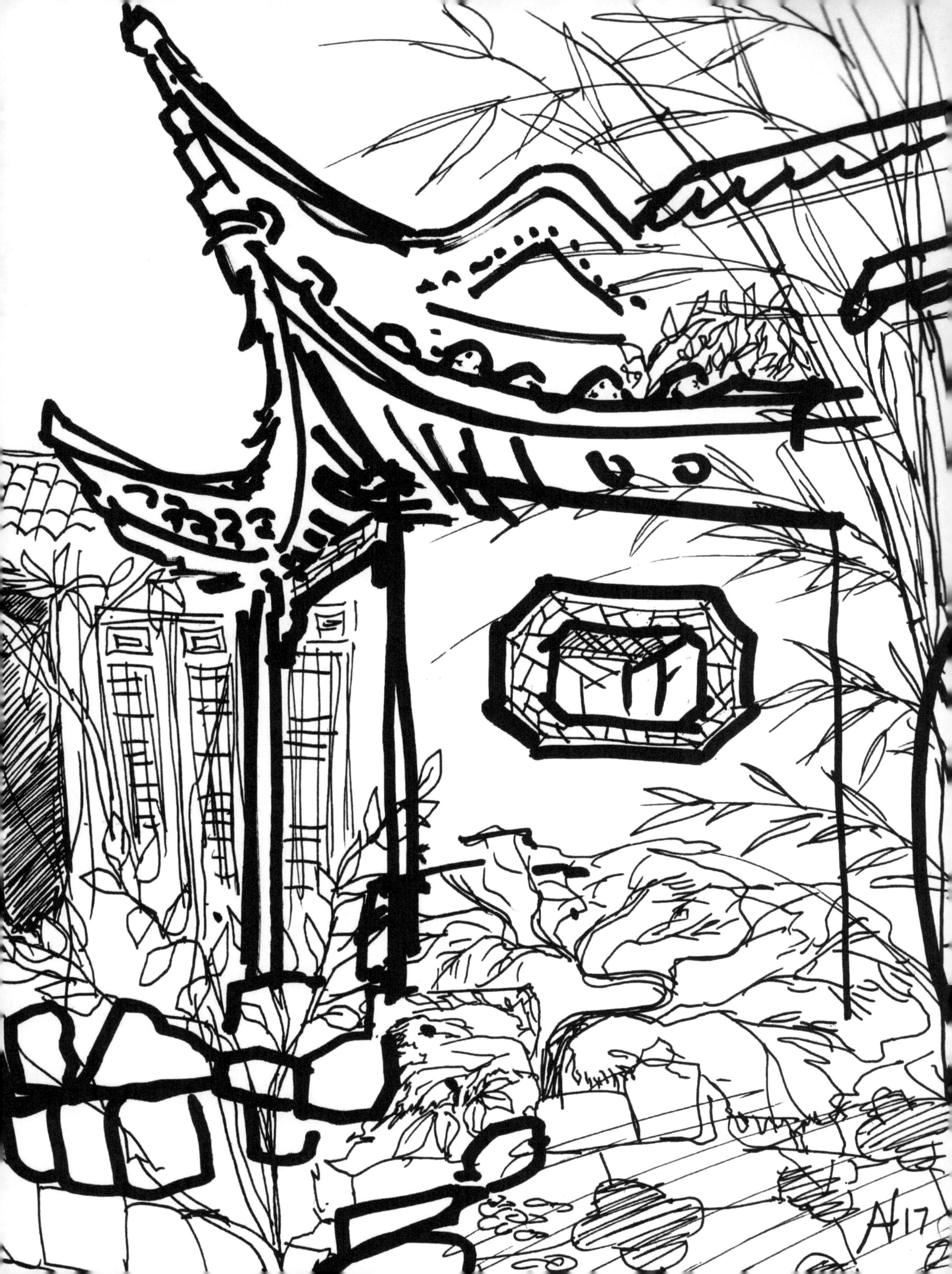

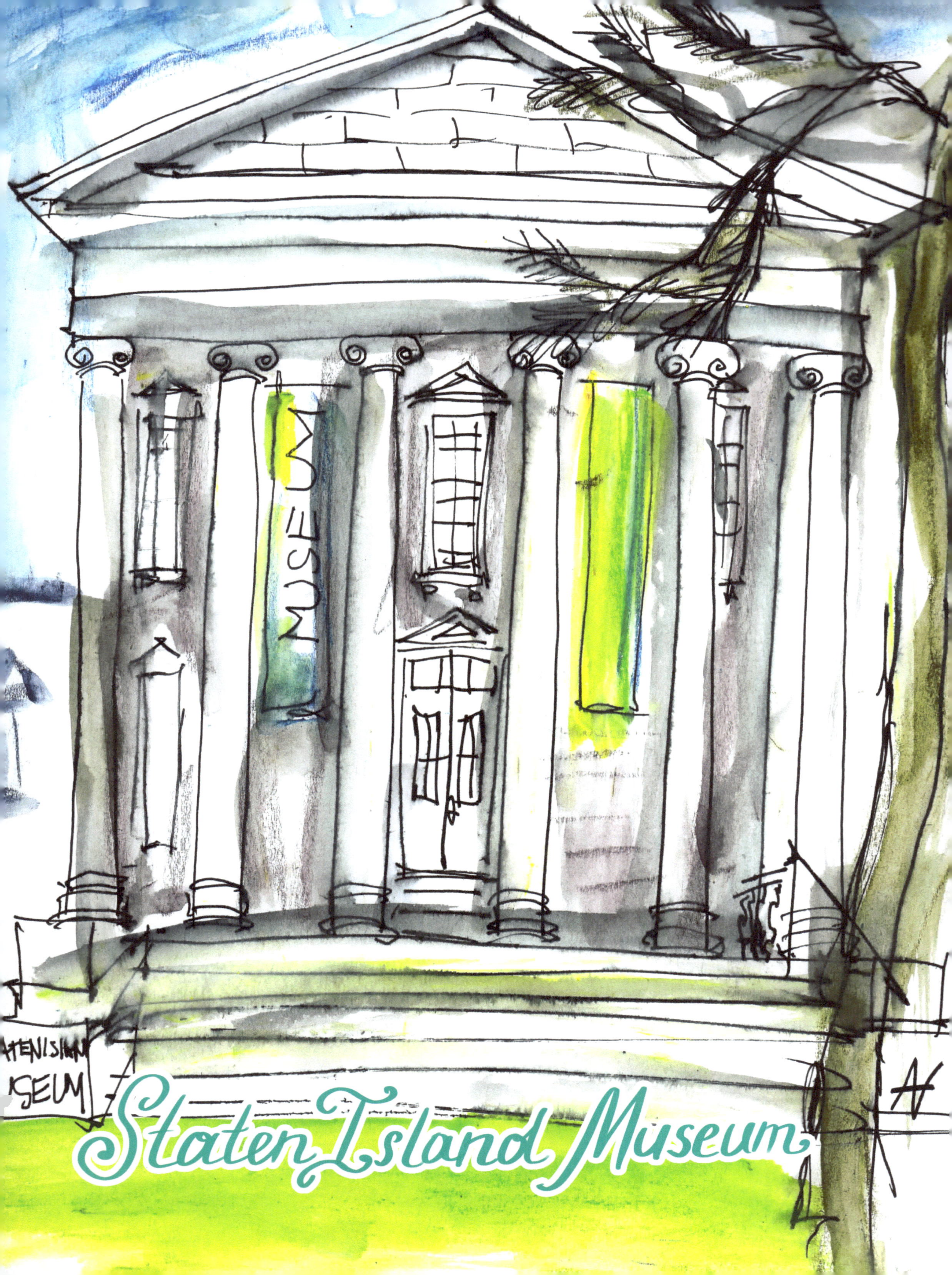

MUSEUM
ATENISLAN
SEUM
Staten Island Museum

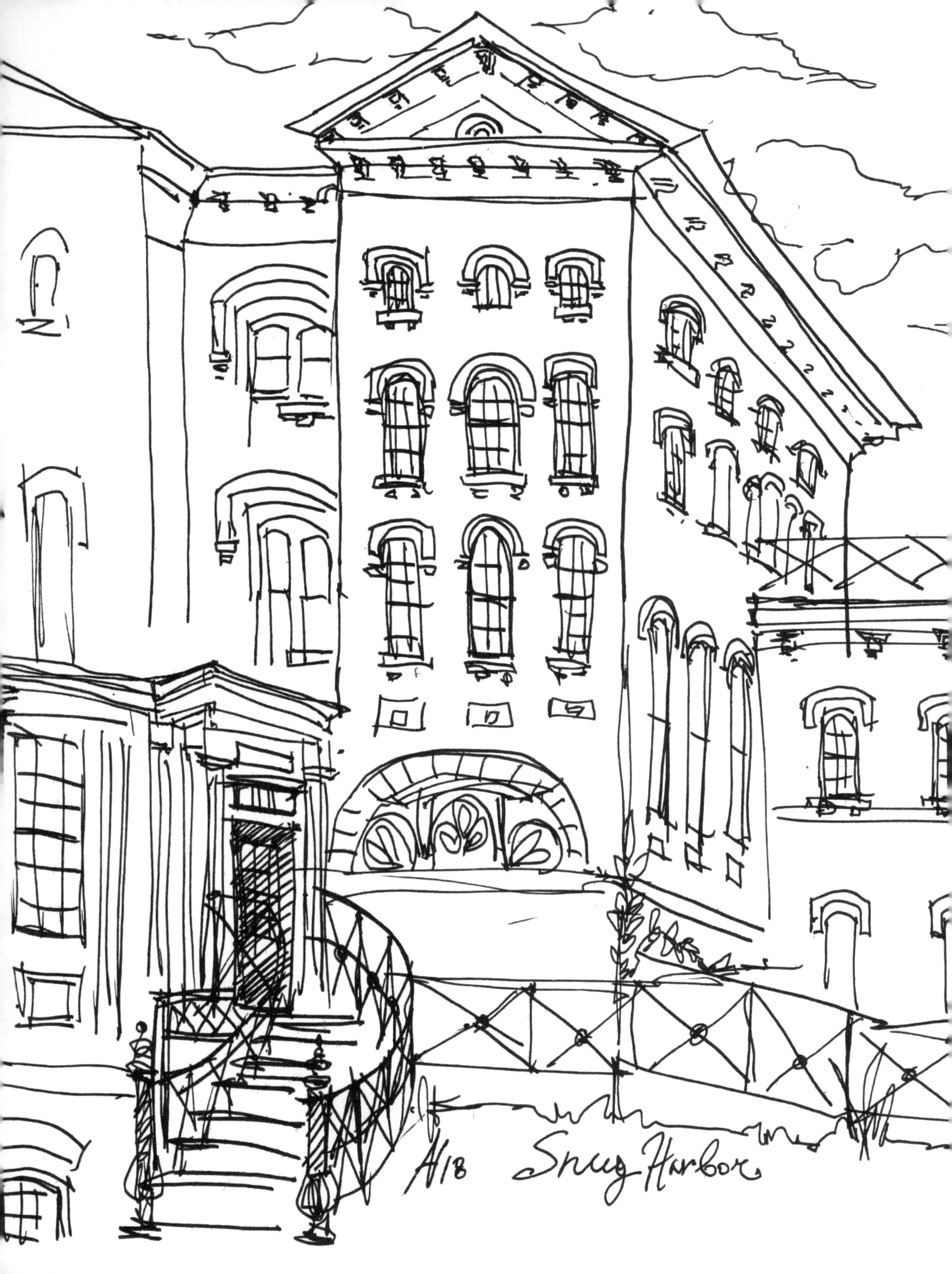
A18 Snug Harbor

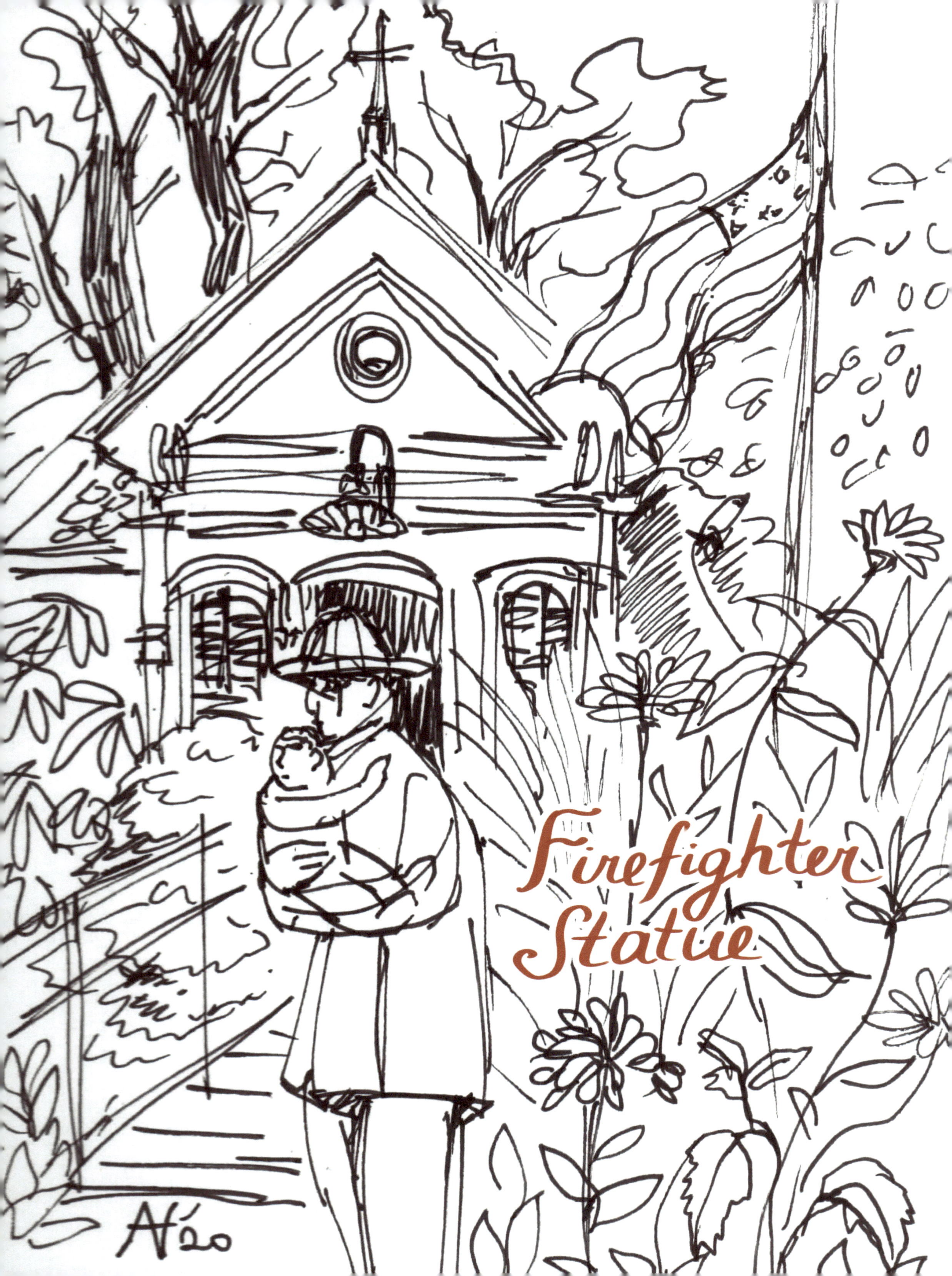

Firefighter
Statue
A'20

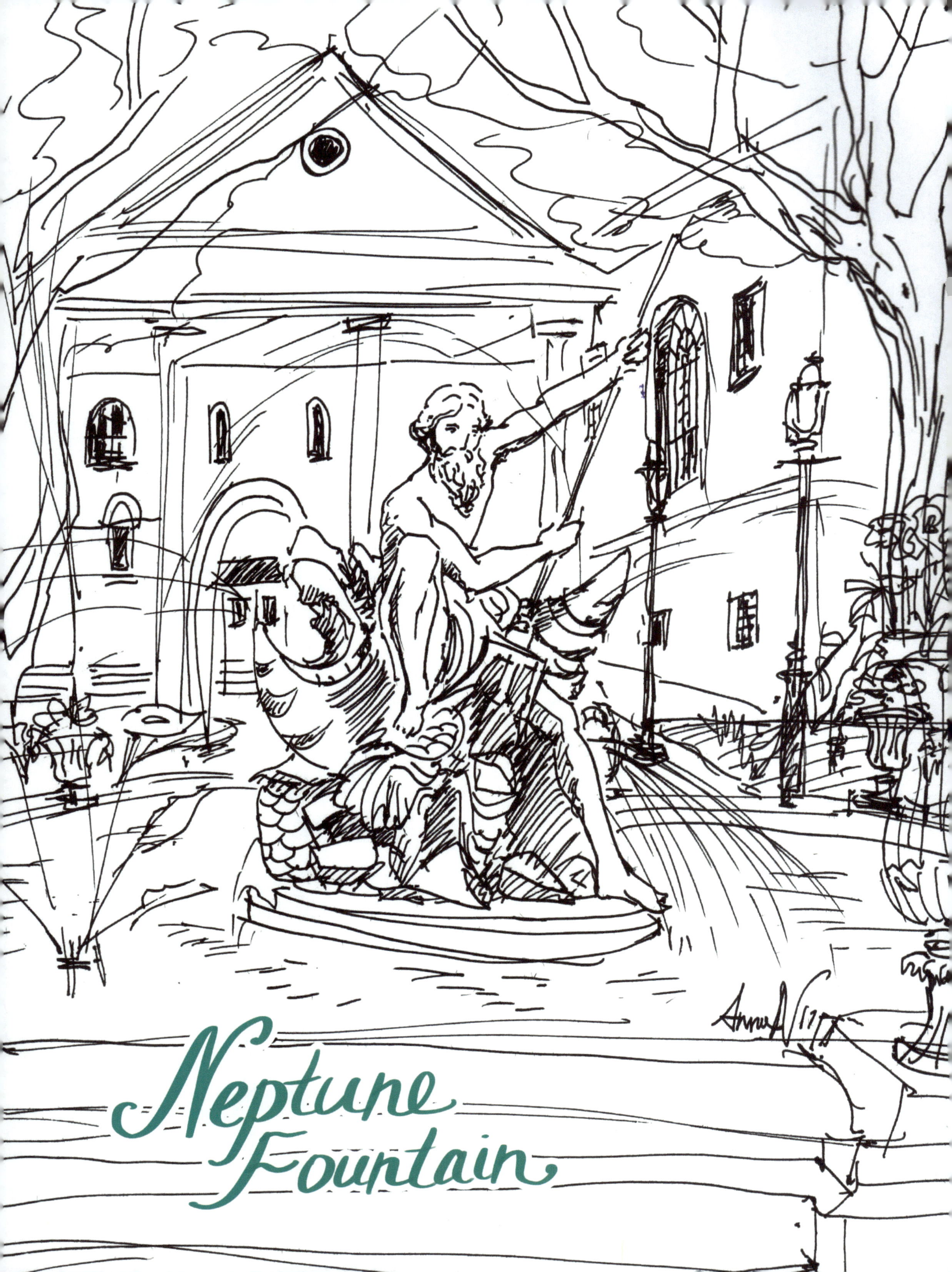

Neptune
Fountain

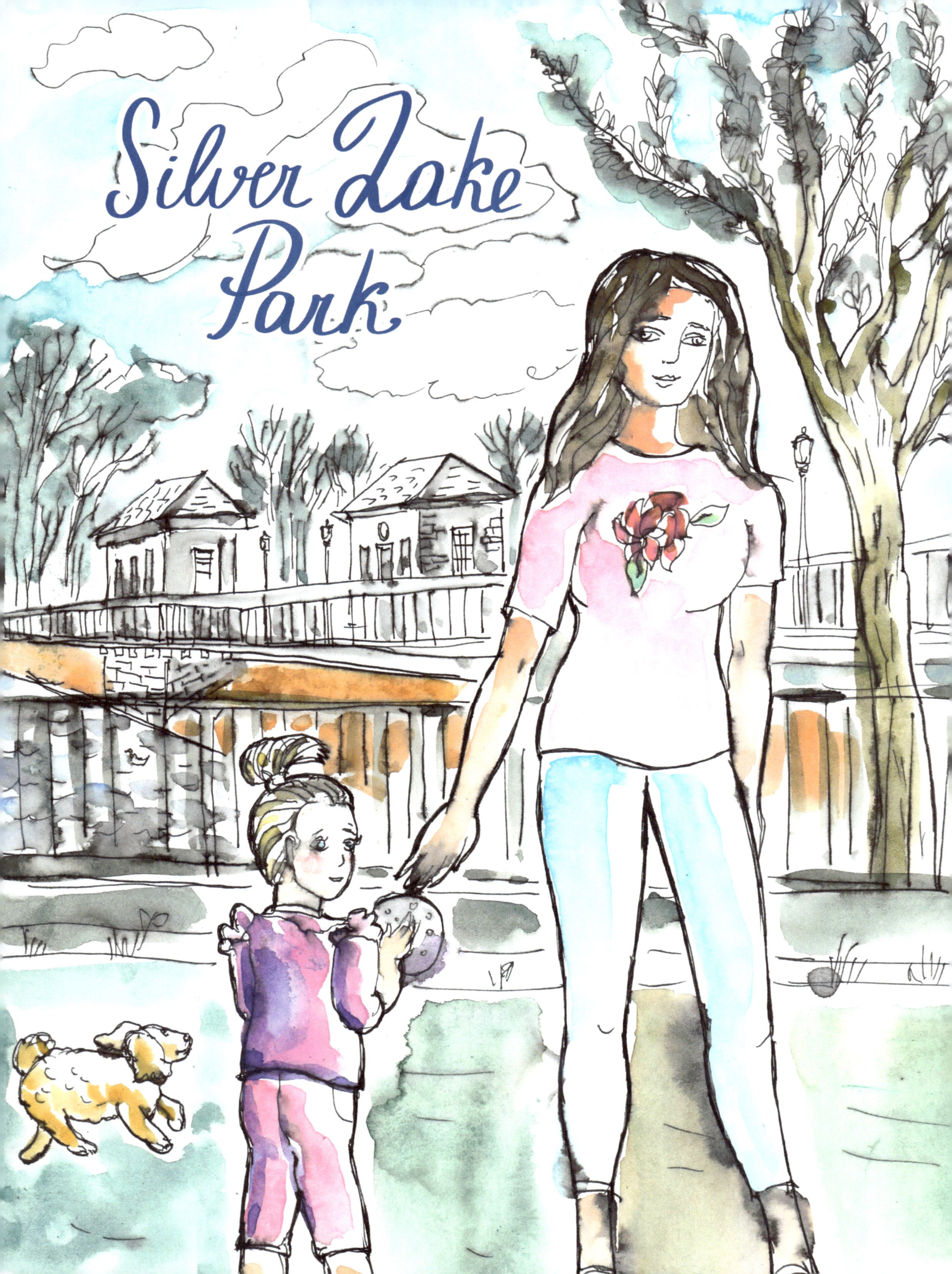

Silver Lake
Park

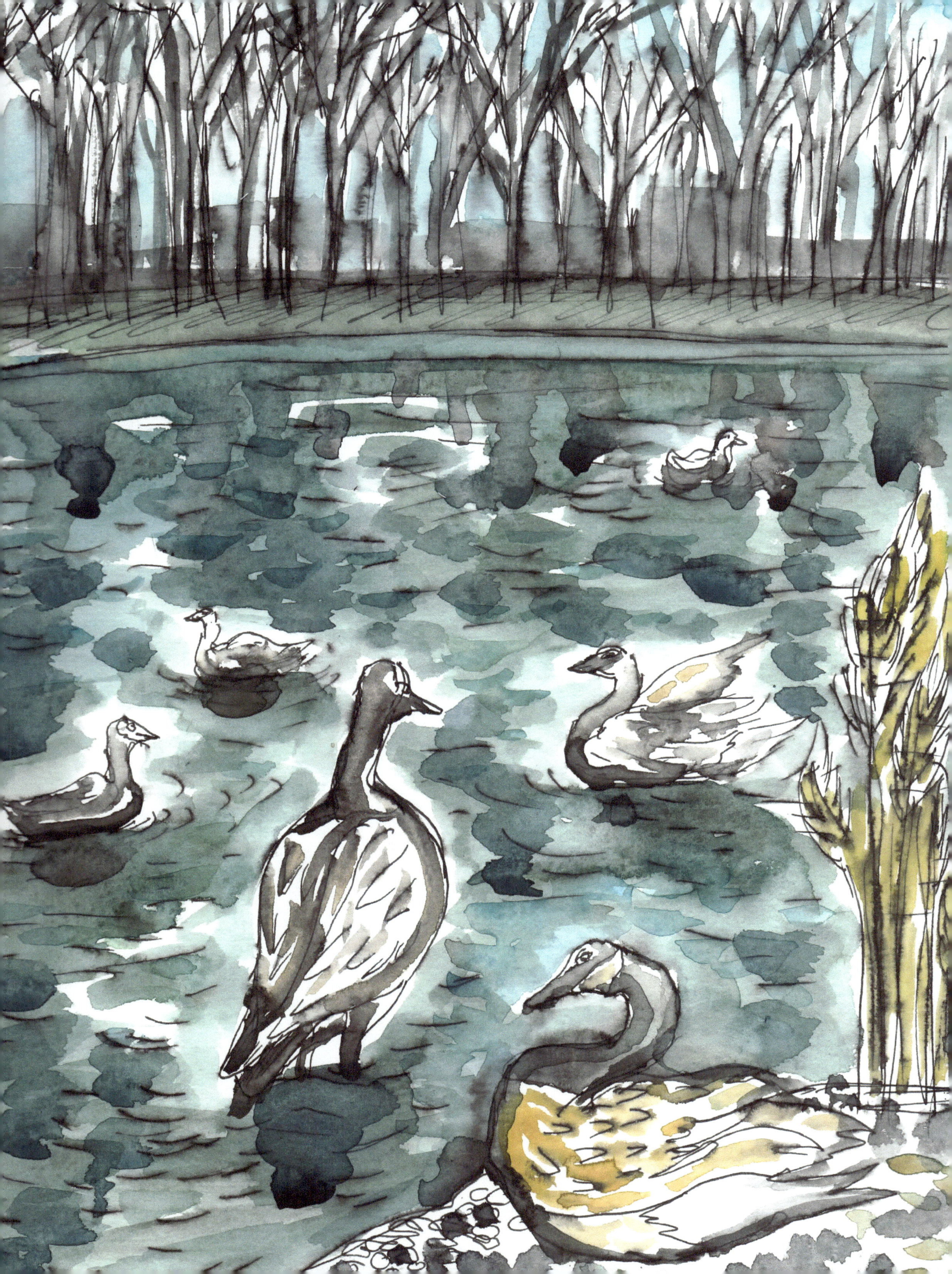

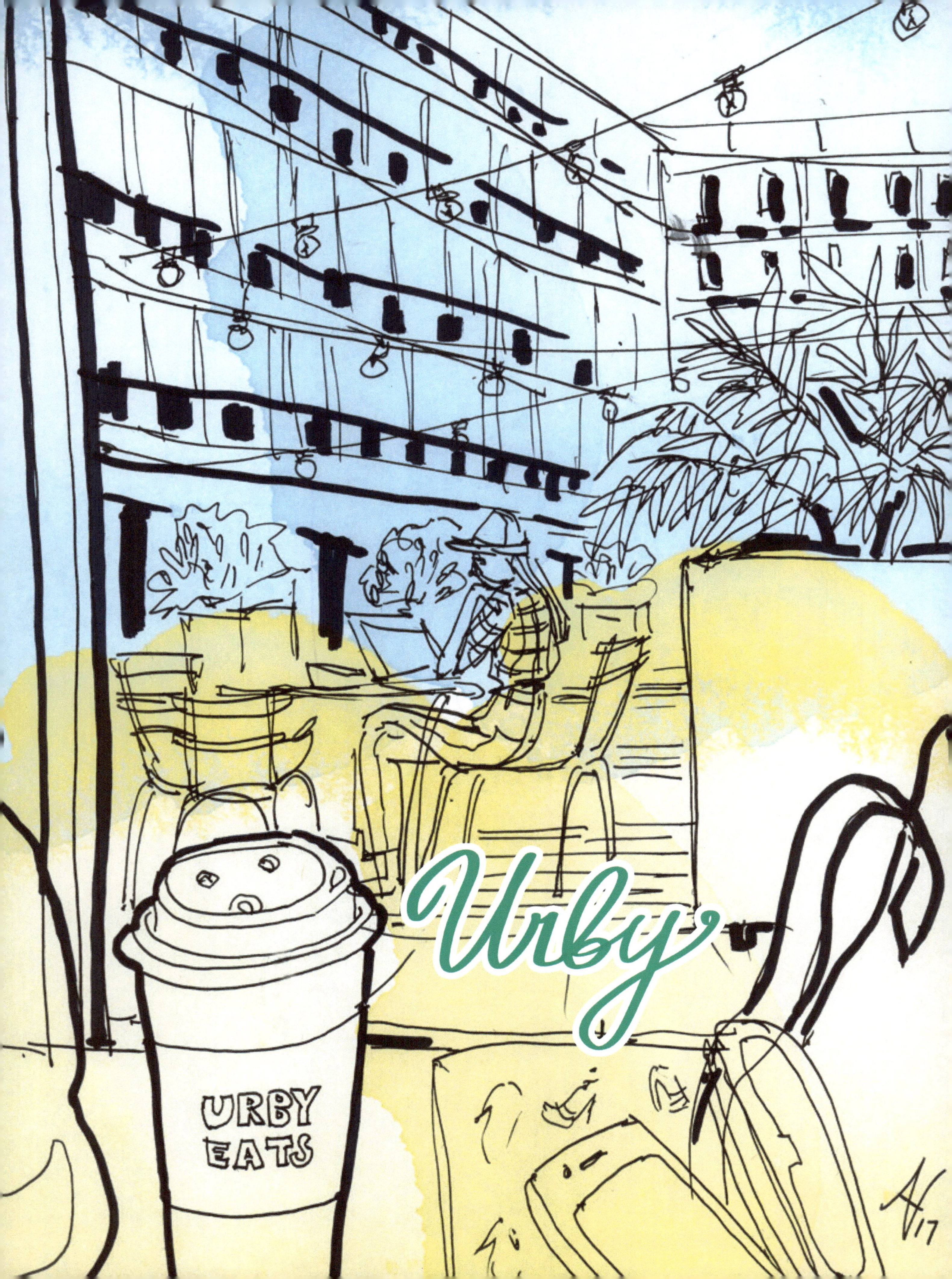

URBY EATS
Urby
'17

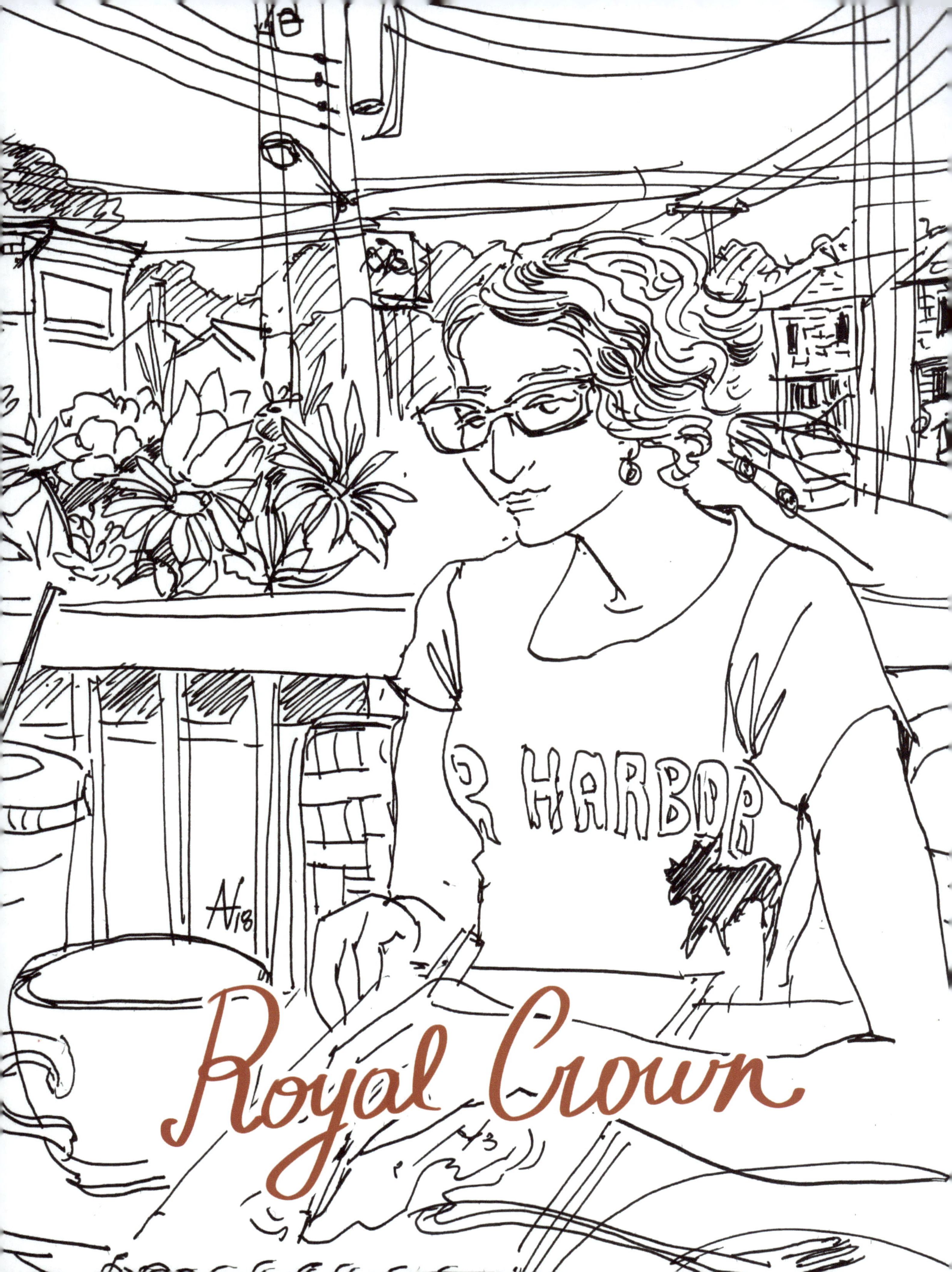
HARBOR
Royal Crown

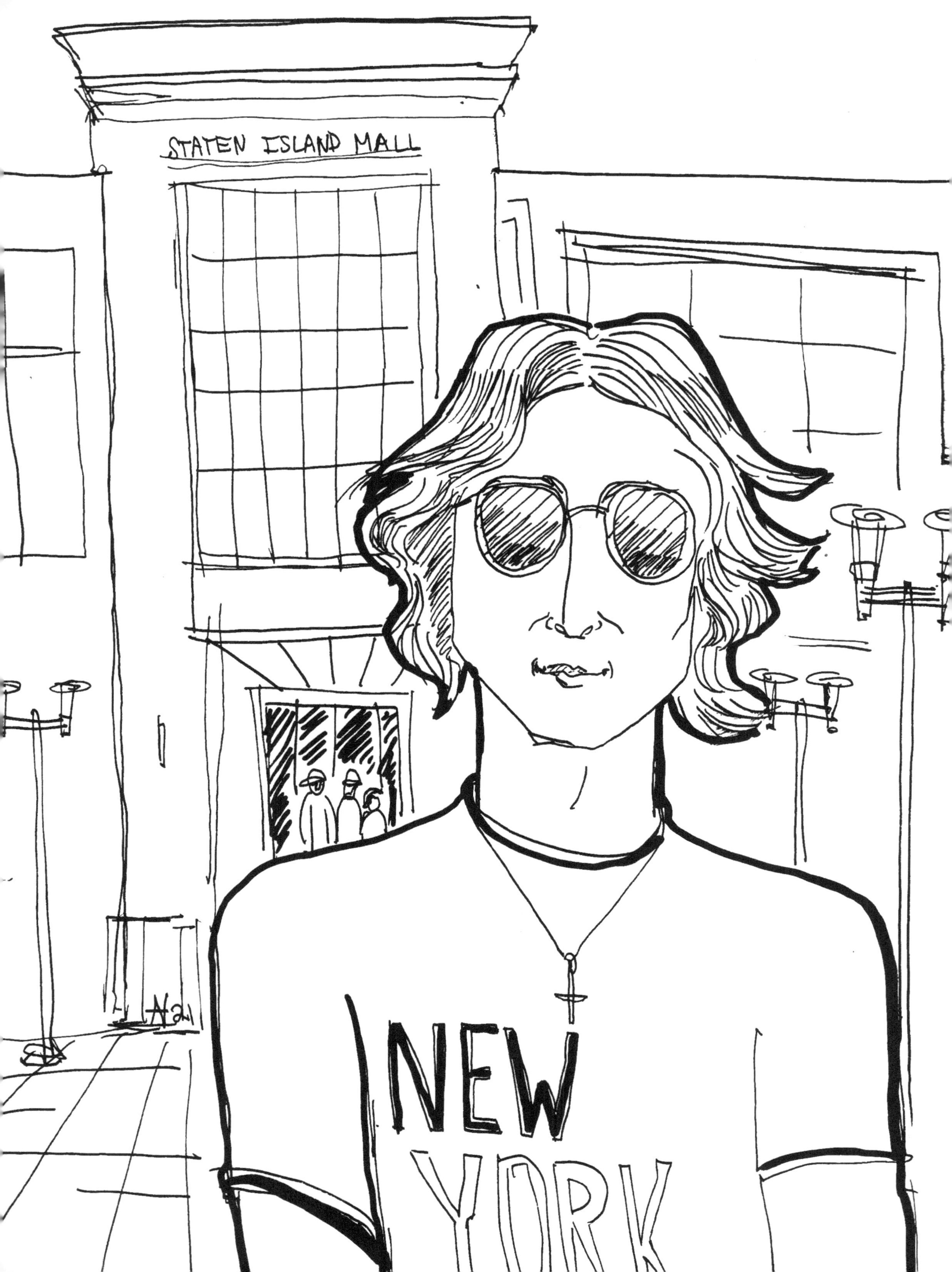
STATEN ISLAND MALL
NEW
YORK

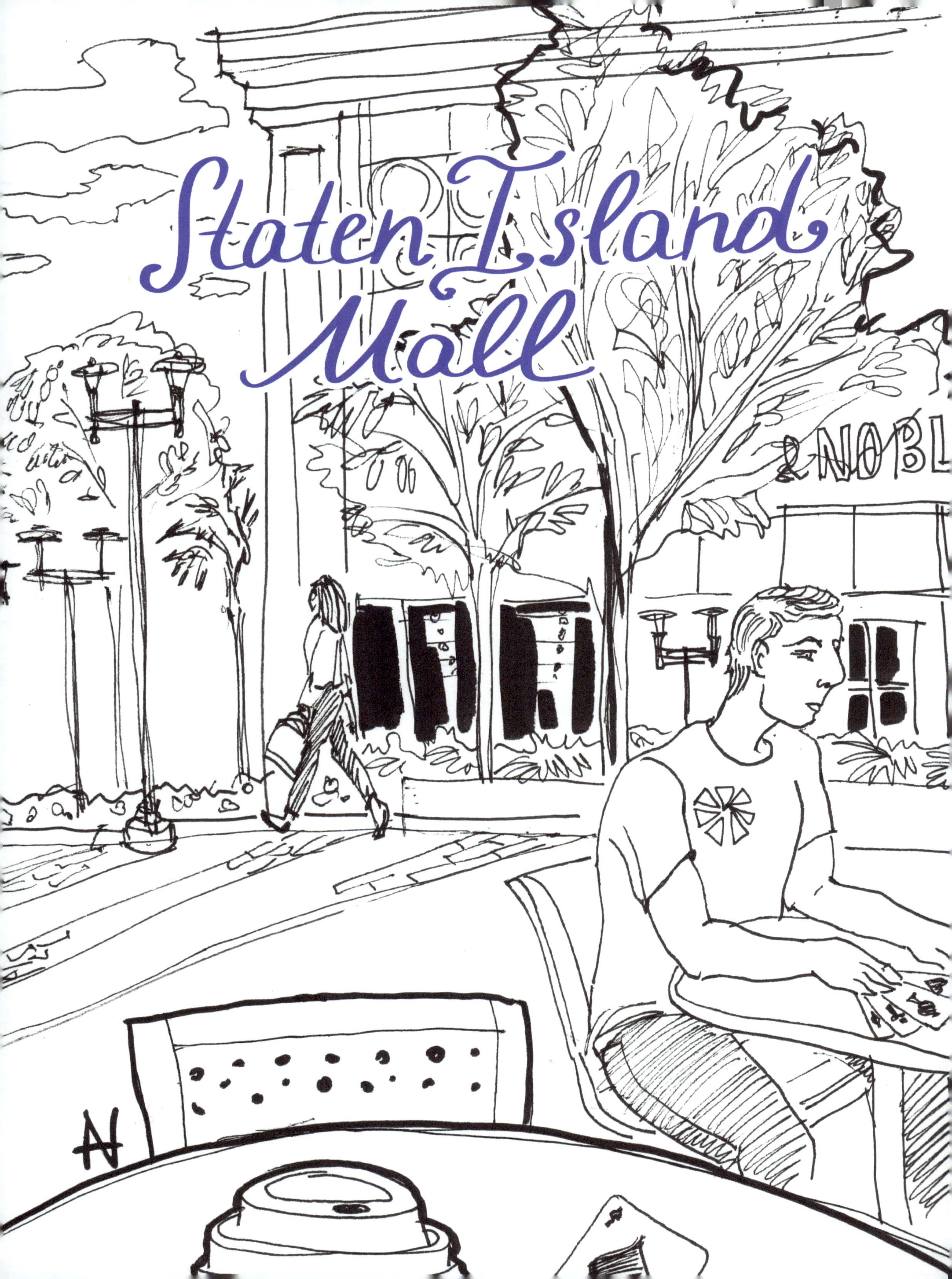

Staten Island Mall
&NOBL

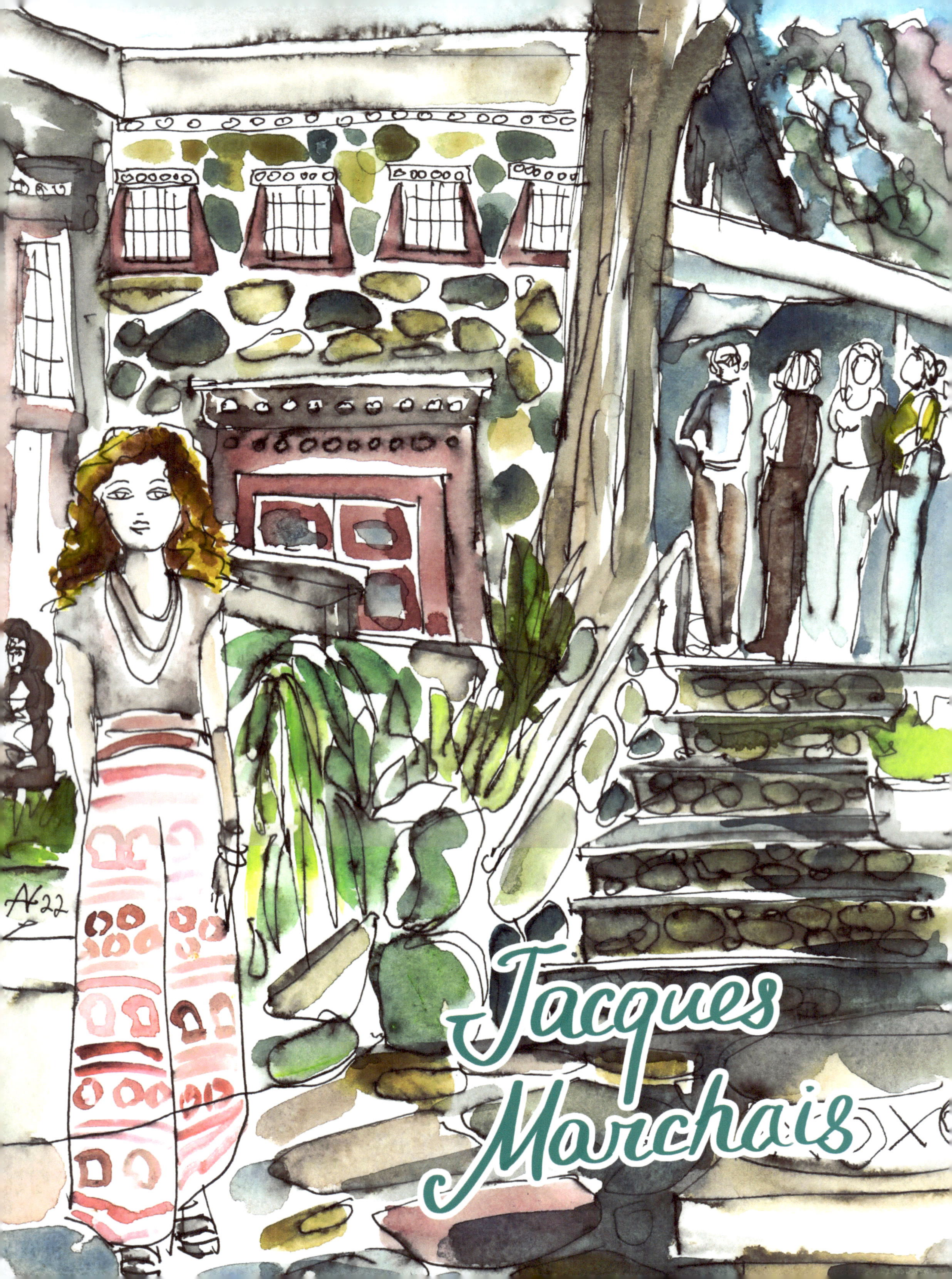
Jacques Marchais

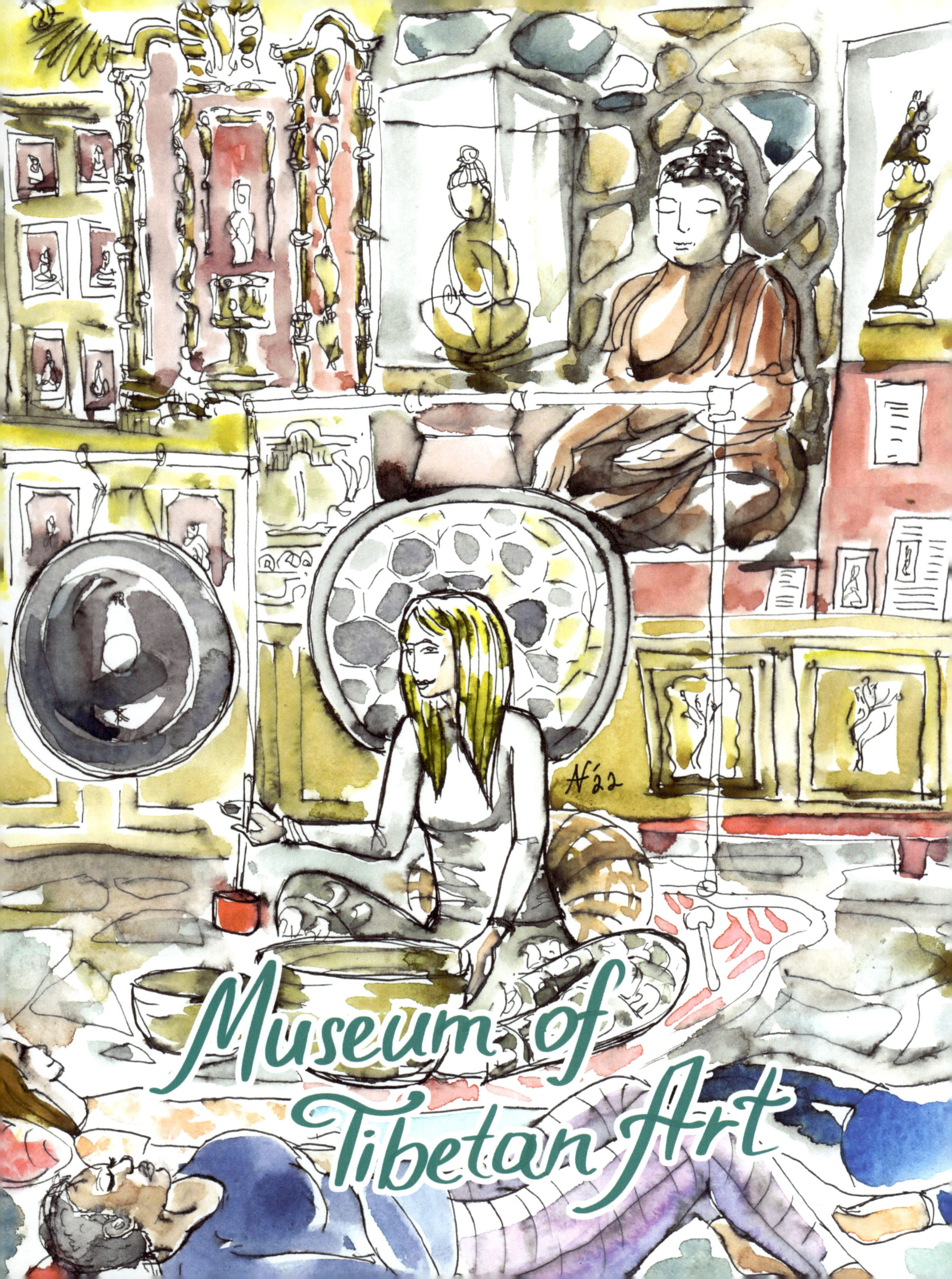
Museum of
Tibetan Art

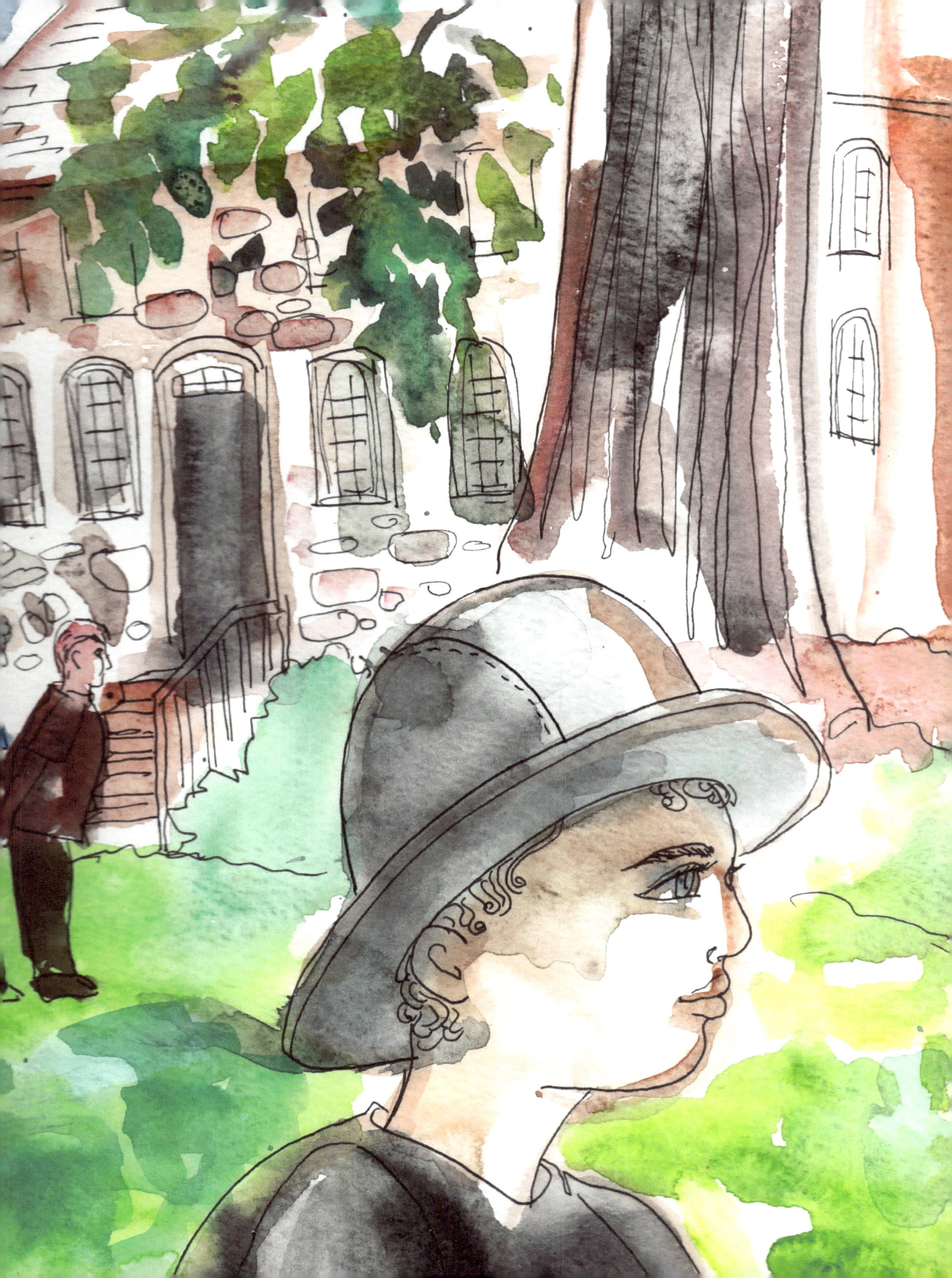

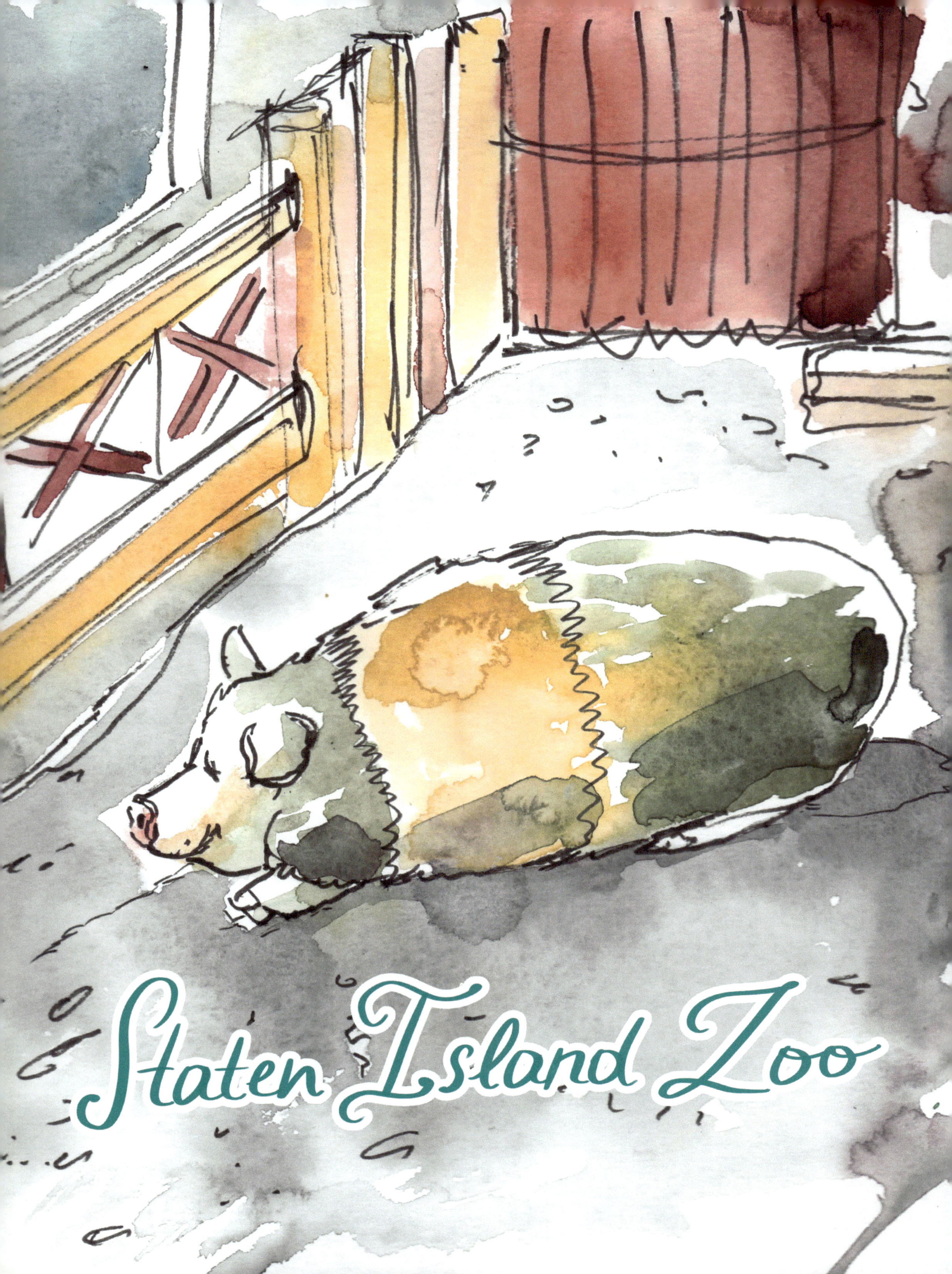
Staten Island Zoo

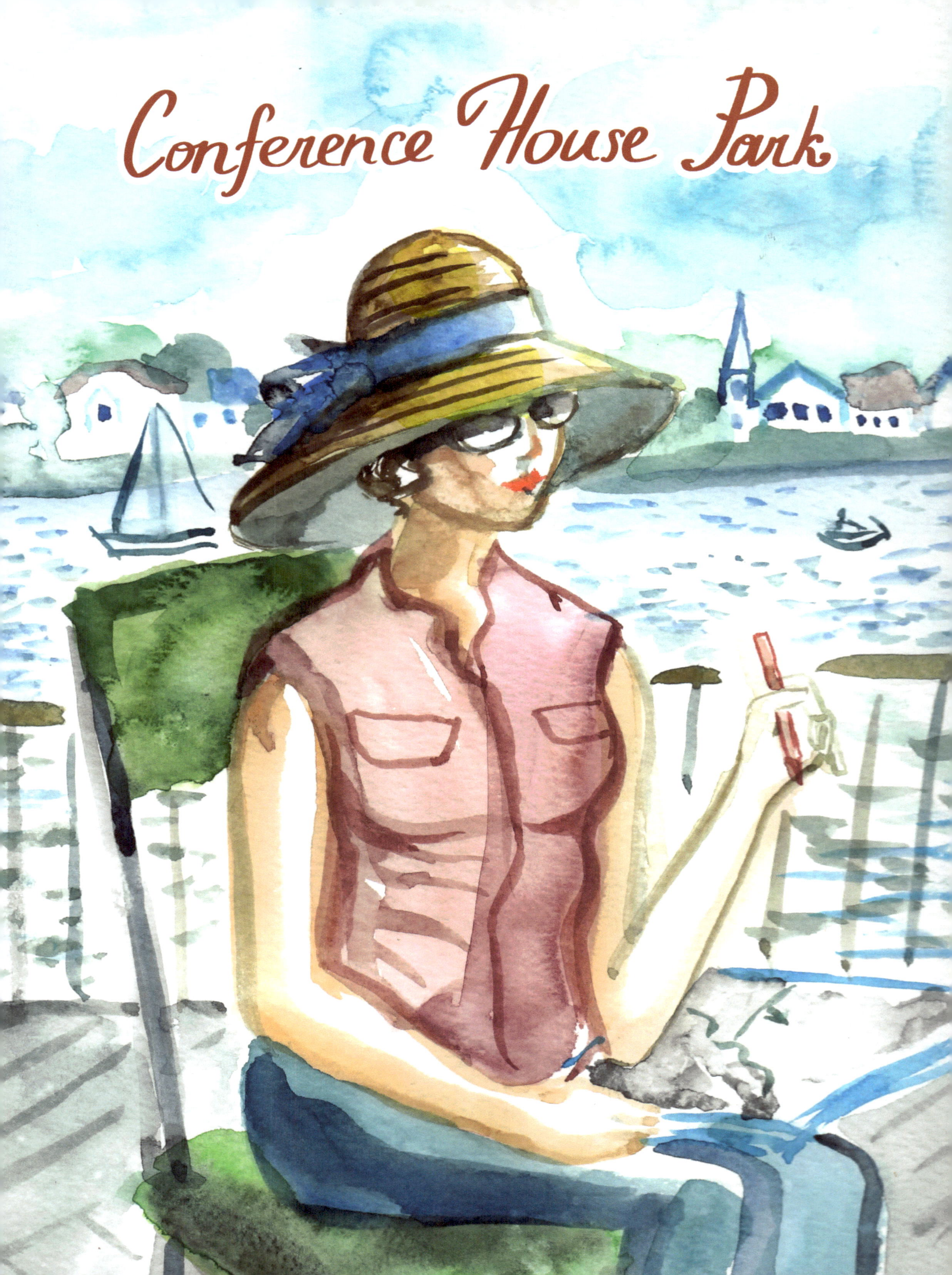

Conference House Park

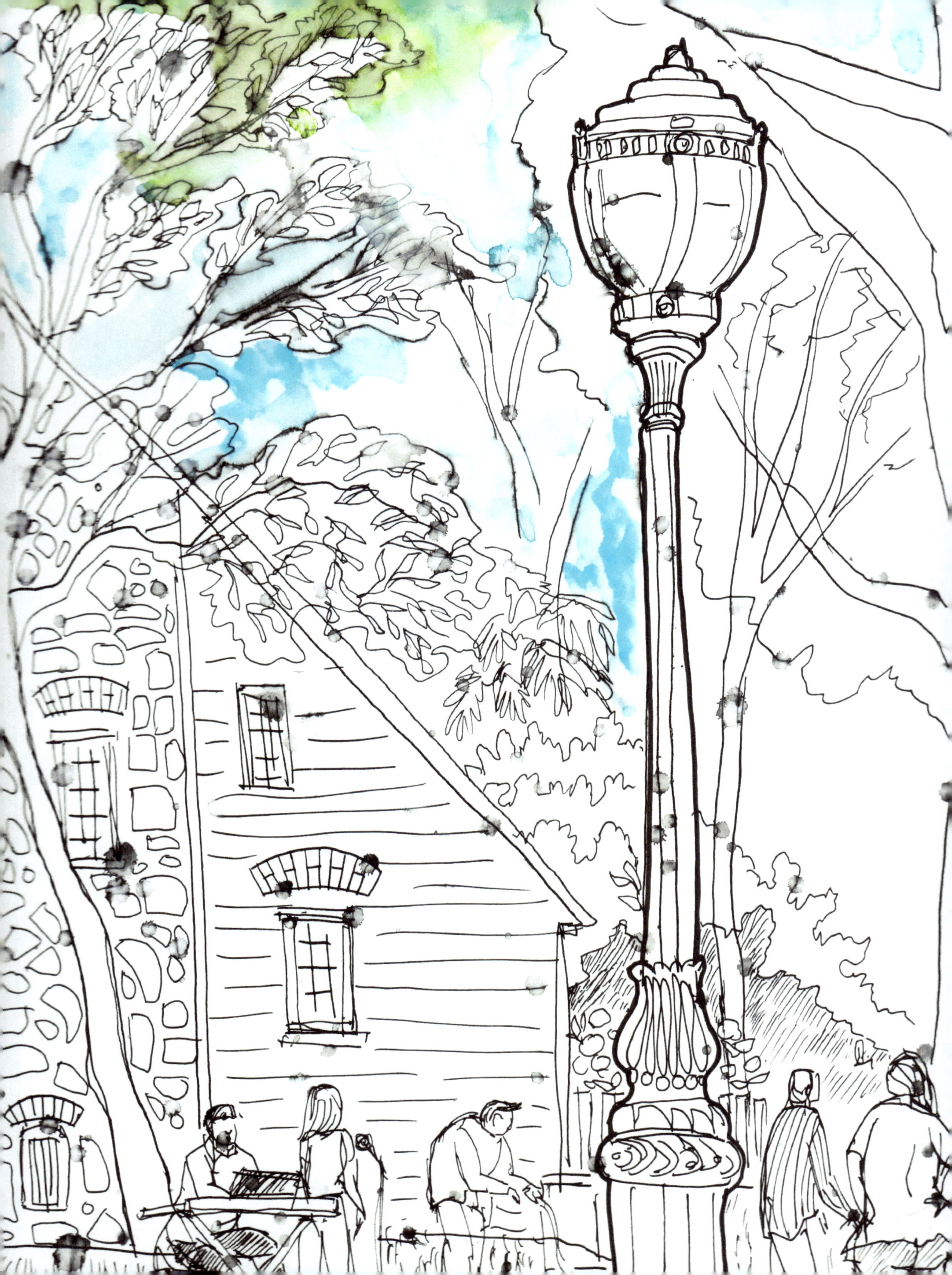

These coloring and picture books
in the "Travel and Cities" Series are
available for purchase on Amazon.

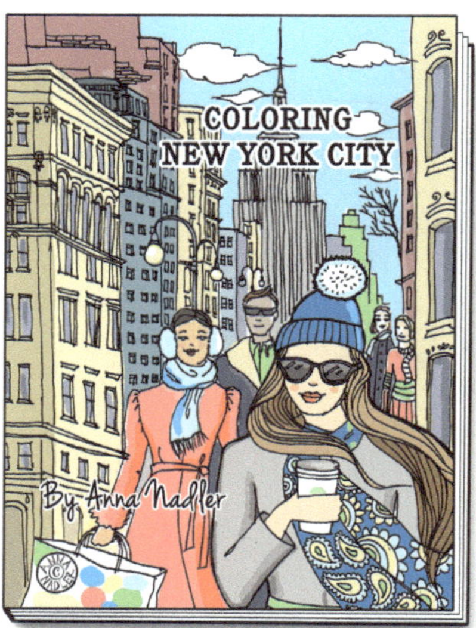

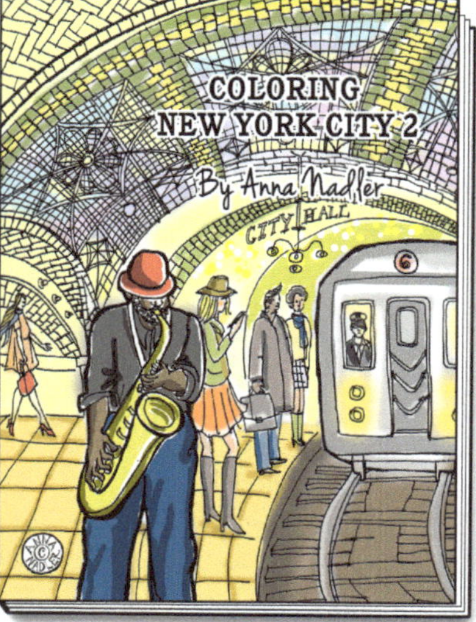

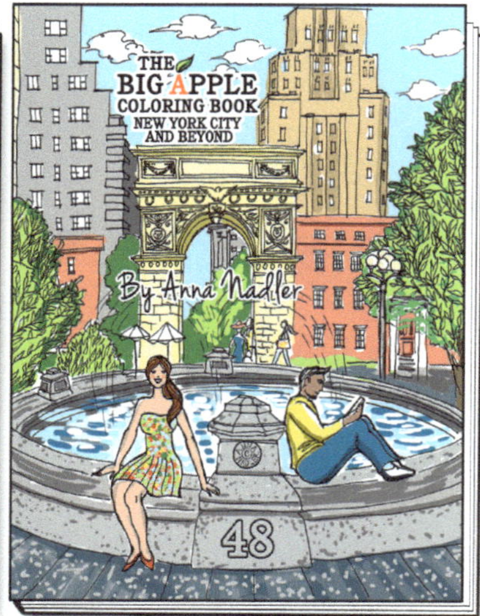

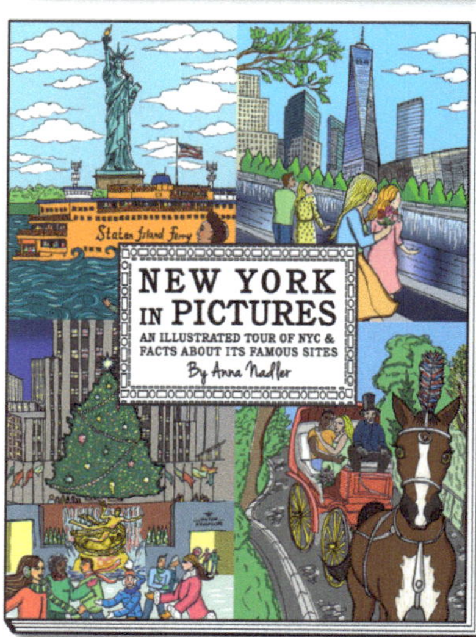

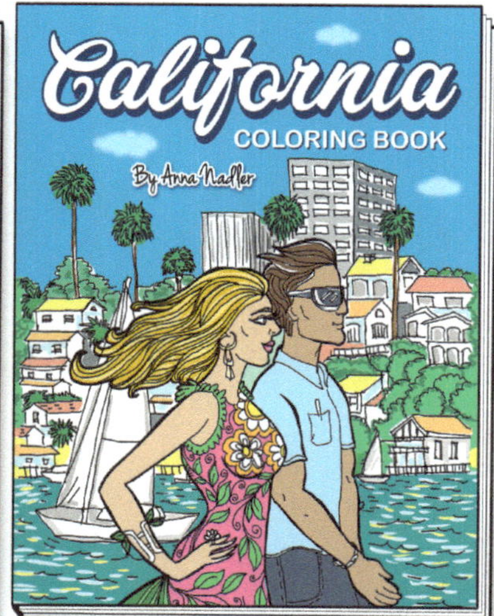

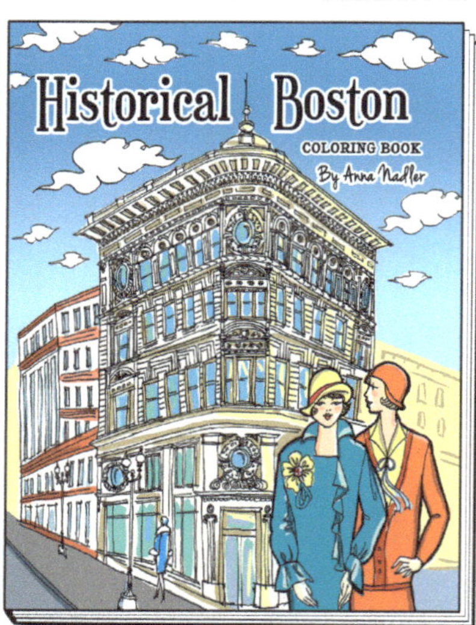

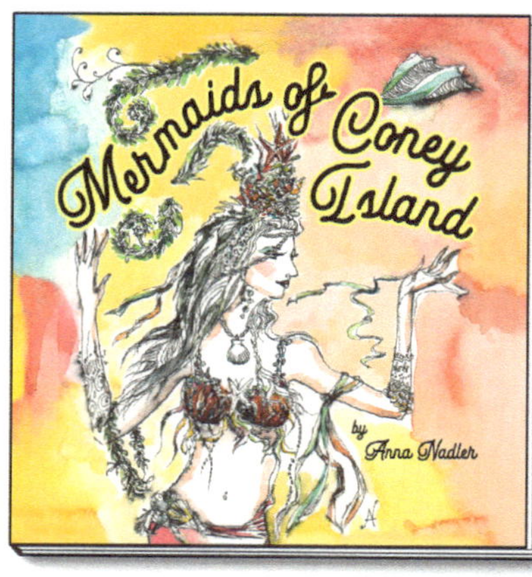

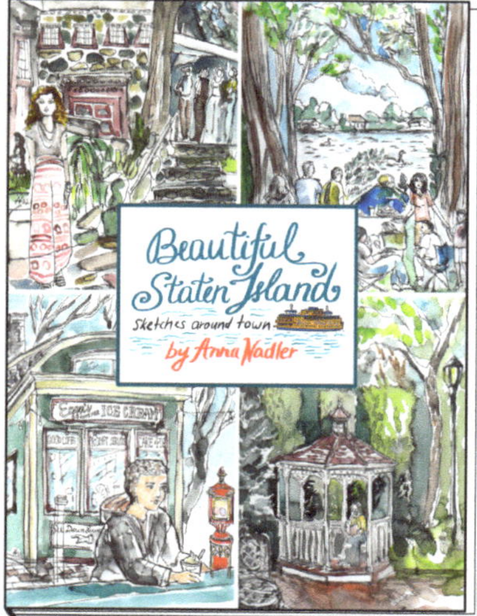

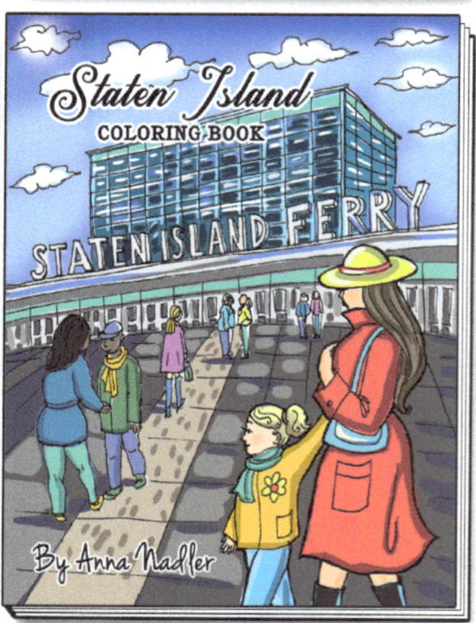

About the Artist

Anna Nadler is an illustrator, graphic designer and author, who lives and works in Staten Island, NY. She loves drawing people, fashion, animals and architecture - trying to capture the unique feeling of every subject she illustrates.
She is always working on new children's books, activity books, coloring books and more.
You can find Anna's books on Amazon and other book retailers.
See more of Anna's illustrations, books, paintings, logo designs, and products on her website - AnnaNadlerArt.com.

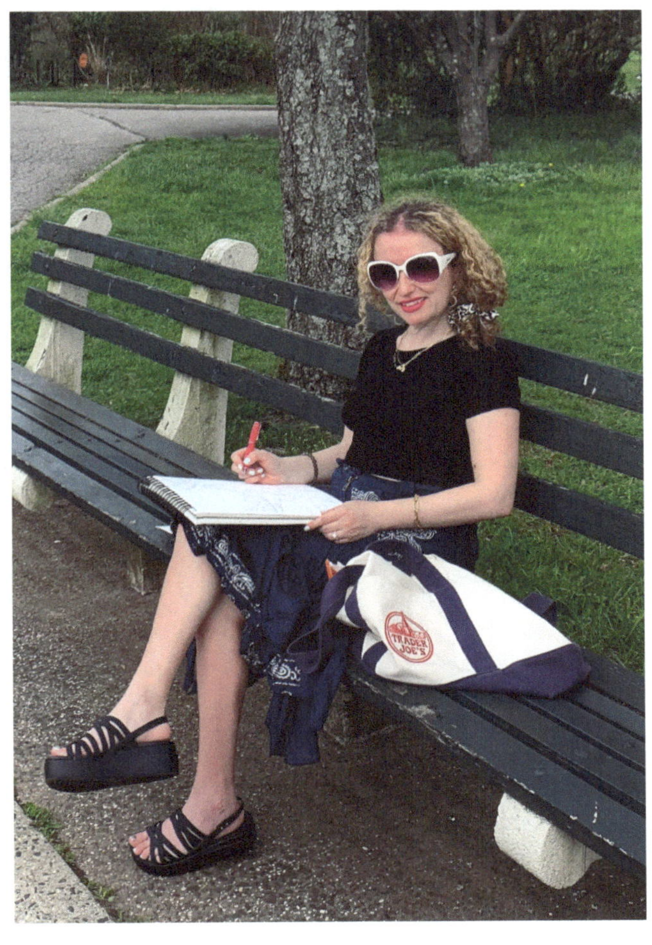

Thank you for getting this book!
If you enjoyed it, please
leave a review!

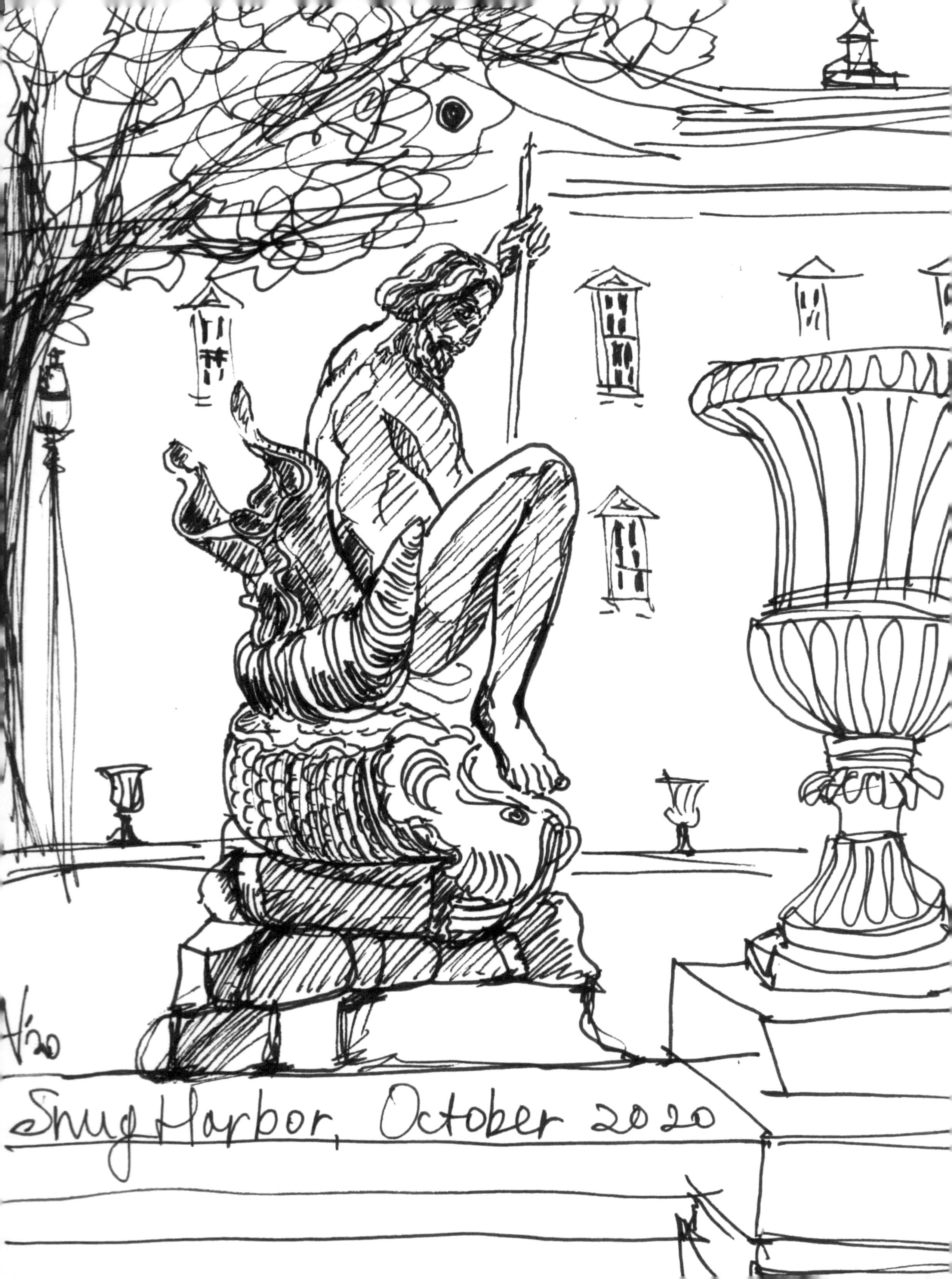

Snug Harbor, October 2020